Fish of New York

FIELD GUIDE

by **Dave Bosanko**

Adventure Publications, Inc.
Cambridge, MN

Edited by Dan Johnson

Cover and book design by Jonathan Norberg

Illustration credits by artist and page number:

Cover illustrations: Brook Trout (main) by Duane Raver/USFWS, Bluegill (upper and back cover) by Joseph Tomelleri

Timothy Knepp/USFWS: 96 (main), 98, 110, 114, 118 **Julie Martinez:** 104, 130 **MyFWC.com/fishing:** 11 **Duane Raver/USFWS:** 10 (both), 11, 19, 22, 24, 26, 28, 30, 32, 34, 40, 42, 44, 48, 50, 52, 62, 80, 88, 100, 102 (main), 108, 134, 150, 152, 154, 156, 158, 162, 164, 166, 172, 174, 176 **Joseph Tomelleri:** 36 (both), 38, 46, 54, 56, 58, 60, 64, 66, 68, 70, 72 (both), 74 (both), 76, 78, 82 (both), 84, 86, 90, 92, 94, 96 (inset), 102 (inset), 106 (both), 112, 116 (all), 120, 122, 124, 126, 128, 132 (both), 136, 138, 140, 142, 144, 146, 148, 160, 168, 170, 178, 180

10 9 8 7 6 5 4 3 2 1
Copyright 2008 by Dave Bosanko
Published by Adventure Publications, Inc.
820 Cleveland St. S
Cambridge, MN 55008
1-800-678-7006
www.adventurepublications.net
ISBN-13: 978-1-59193-078-5
ISBN-10: 1-59193-078-2

TABLE OF CONTENTS

4

HOW TO USE THIS BOOK

Your *Fish of New York Field Guide* is designed to make it easy to identify more than 80 species of the most common and important fish in New York, and learn fascinating facts about each species' range, natural history and more.

The fish are organized by families, such as Catfish (*Ictaluridae*), Perch (*Percidae*), Trout and Salmon (*Salmonidae*) and Sunfish (*Centrarchidae*), which are listed in alphabetical order. Within these families, individual species are arranged alphabetically in their appropriate groups. For example, members of the Sunfish family are divided into Black Bass, Crappie and True Sunfish groups. For a detailed list of fish families and individual species, turn to the Table of Contents (page 3); the Index (page 186–191) provides a reference guide to fish by common name (such as Lake Trout) and other common terms for the species.

Fish Identification

Determining a fish's body shape is the first step to identifying it. Each fish family usually exhibits one or sometimes two basic outlines. Catfish have long, stout bodies with flattened heads, barbels or "whiskers" around the mouth, a relatively tall but narrow dorsal fin and an adipose fin. There are two forms of Sunfish: the flat, round, plate-like outline we see in Bluegills; and the torpedo or "fusiform" shape of Largemouth Bass.

In this field guide you can quickly identify a fish by first matching its general body shape to one of the fish family silhouettes listed in the Table of Contents (pp. 3–7). From there, turn to that family's section and use the illustrations and text descriptions to identify your fish. Example Pages (pp. 22–23) are provided to explain how the information is presented in each two-page spread.

For some species, the illustration will be enough to identify your catch, but it is important to note that your fish may not look exactly like the artwork. Fish frequently change colors. Males that are brightly colored during the spawning season may show muted coloration at other times. Likewise, bass caught in muddy streams show much less pattern than those taken from clear lakes—and all fish lose some of their markings and color when removed from the water.

Most fish are similar in appearance to one or more other species—often, but not always, within the same family. For example, the Black Crappie is remarkably similar to the White Crappie. To accurately identify such look-alikes, check the inset illustrations and accompanying notes below the main illustration, under the "Similar Species" heading.

Throughout *Fish of New York* we use basic biological and fisheries management terms that refer to physical characteristics or conditions of fish and their environment, such as *dorsal* fin or *turbid* water. For your convenience, these are listed and defined in the Glossary (pp. 182–185), along with other handy fish-related terms and their definitions.

Understanding such terminology will help you make sense of reports on state and federal research, fish population surveys, lake assessments, management plans and other important fisheries documents.

FISH ANATOMY

It's much easier to identify fish if you know the names of different parts of a fish. For example, it's easier to use the term "adipose fin" to indicate the small, soft, fleshy flap on a Rainbow Trout's back than try to describe it. The following illustrations point out the basic parts of a fish; the accompanying text defines these characteristics.

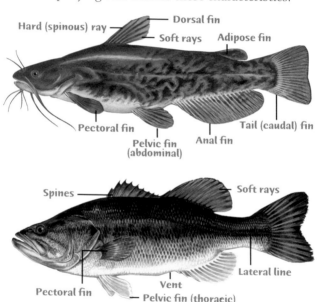

Fins are made up of bony structures that support a membrane. There are three kinds of bony structures in fins:
Soft rays are flexible fin supports and are often branched.

Spines are stiff, often sharp supports that are not jointed. **Hard rays** are stiff, pointed, barbed structures that can be raised or lowered. Catfish are famous for their hard rays, which are often mistakenly called spines. Sunfish have soft rays associated with spines to form a prominent dorsal fin.

Fins are named by their position on the fish. The **dorsal fin** is on top along the midline. A few species have another fin on their back, called an **adipose fin**. This small, fleshy protuberance located between the dorsal fin and the tail is distinctive of catfish, trout and salmon. **Pectoral fins** are found on each side of the fish near the gills. The **anal fin** is located along the midline, on the fish's bottom or *ventral* side. There is also a paired set of fins on the bottom of the fish, called the **pelvic fins**. These can be in the **thoracic position** (just below the pectoral fins) or farther back on the stomach, in the **abdominal position**. The tail is known as the **caudal fin**.

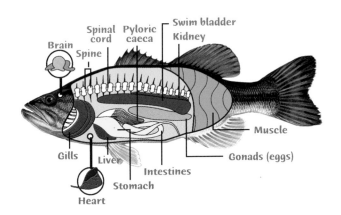

11

Eyes—A fish's eyes can detect color. Their eyes are rounder than those of mammals because of the refractive index of water; focus is achieved by moving the lens in and out, not distorting it as in mammals. Different species have varying levels of eyesight. Walleyes see well in low light. Bluegills have excellent daytime vision but see poorly at night, making them vulnerable to predation.

Nostrils—A pair of nostrils, or *nares*, are used to detect odors in the water. Eels and catfishes have particularly well-developed senses of smell.

Mouth—The shape of the mouth is a clue to what the fish eats. The larger the food it consumes, the larger the mouth.

Teeth—Not all fish have teeth, but those that do have mouthgear designed to help them feed. Walleyes, Northern Pike and Tiger Muskies have sharp *canine* teeth for grabbing and holding prey. Minnows have *pharyngeal* teeth—located in the throat—for grinding.

Catfish have *cardiform* teeth, which feel like a rough patch in the front of the mouth. Bass have patches of *vomerine* teeth on the roof of their mouth.

Swim Bladder—Almost all fish have a swim bladder, a balloon-like organ that helps the fish regulate its buoyancy.

Lateral Line—This sensory organ helps the fish detect movement in the water (to help avoid predators or capture prey) as well as water currents and pressure changes. It consists of fluid-filled sacs with hair-like sensors, which are open to the water through a row of pores in their skin along each side—creating a visible line along the fish's side.

FISH NAMES

A Walleye is a Walleye in New York. But in the northern parts of its range, Canadians call it a jack or jackfish. In some areas it is often called a pickerel or walleyed pike.

Because common names may vary regionally, and even change for different sizes of the same species, scientific names are used that are exactly the same around the world. Each species has only one correct scientific name that can be recognized anywhere, in any language. The Walleye is *Sander vitreus* from Buffalo to Berlin.

Scientific names are made up of Greek or Latin words that often describe the species. There are two parts to a scientific name: the generic or "genus," which is capitalized (*Sander*), and the specific name, which is not capitalized (*vitreus*). Both are displayed in italic text.

A species' genus represents a group of closely related fish. The Walleye and Sauger are in the same genus, so they share the generic name *Sander*. But each have different specific names, *vitreus* for Walleye, *canadense* for the Sauger.

ABOUT NEW YORK FISH

New York is the largest state in the Northeast and also the most diverse when it comes to freshwater fish. Of the approximately 163 freshwater species found in the Northeast, 160 reside in New York. This can be compared to Maine, nearly the same size, which has only 64 species. Added to this are the 30 or so marine species that migrate into freshwater to spawn.

This diversity of fishes is directly due to the diversity of freshwater habitats found within New York's boundaries: the large "inland seas"—lakes Erie and Ontario; the deep, clear lakes like Champlain and the Finger Lakes; the beautiful mountain lakes in the Adirondacks; and the hundreds of not-so-clear, small ponds and lakes scattered across central New York.

New York is also blessed with an extensive river system. We have everything from small, fast, mountain brooks through the sluggish streams of Long Island to the mighty St. Lawrence and Hudson rivers that flow to the sea.

Of all of these, the most important to fish diversity is the Allegheny drainage. It is through the Allegheny system—which is connected to the Ohio River—that over 60 fish species from the Mississippi River drainage reach New York. All of these water systems are supported by more than 40 inches of rain per year.

The fish in this book represent the 30 or so species that are targeted by recreational fishermen and another 50 species that are of particular interest to those who spend time near the water, either because of their status as baitfish or some unique or interesting characteristic.

FREQUENTLY ASKED QUESTIONS

What is a fish?

Fish are aquatic, typically cold-blooded animals that have backbones, gills and fins.

Are all fish cold-blooded?

All freshwater fish are cold-blooded. Recently it has been discovered that some members of the saltwater Tuna family are warm-blooded. Whales and Bottlenose Dolphins are also warm-blooded, but they are mammals, not fish.

Do all fish have scales?

No. Most fish have scales that look like those on the Common Goldfish. A few, such as Alligator Gar, have scales that resemble armor plates. Catfish have no scales at all.

How do fish breathe?

A fish takes in water through its mouth and forces it through its gills, where a system of fine membranes absorbs oxygen from the water and releases carbon dioxide. Gills cannot pump air efficiently over these membranes, which quickly dry out and stick together. Fish should never be out of the water longer than you can hold your breath.

Can fish breathe air?

Some species can; gars have a modified swim bladder that acts like a lung. Fish that can't breathe air may die when dissolved oxygen in the water falls below critical levels.

How do fish swim?

Fish swim by contracting bands of muscles on alternate sides of their body so the tail is whipped rapidly from side to side. Pectoral and pelvic fins are used mainly for stability when a fish hovers, but are sometimes used during rapid bursts of forward motion.

Do all fish look like fish?

Most do and are easily recognizable as fish. The eels and lampreys are fish, but they look like snakes. Sculpins look like little goblins with bat wings.

Where can you find fish?

Some fish species can be found in almost any body of water, but not all fish are found everywhere. Each is designed to exploit a particular habitat. A species may move around within its home water, sometimes migrating hundreds of miles between lakes, rivers and tributary streams. Some movements, such as spawning migrations, are seasonal and very predictable.

Fish may also move horizontally from one area to another, or vertically in the water column, in response to changes in environmental conditions and food availability. In addition, many fish have daily travel patterns. By studying a species' habitat, food and spawning information in this book—and understanding how it interacts with other New York fish—it is possible to make an educated prediction of where to find it in any lake, stream or river.

FISH DISEASES

Fish are susceptible to various parasites, infections and diseases. One of the newest threats is viral hemorrhagic septicemia (VHS) virus, a serious pathogen of fresh and saltwater fish that is causing an emerging disease in the Great Lakes region of the United States and Canada. VHS virus affects fish of all size and age ranges. It does not pose a threat to human health, but VHS has been blamed for fish kills in lakes Huron, St. Clair, Erie, Ontario, Conesus and Skaneateles, and the St. Lawrence River.

In June 2007 fish health regulations were finalized to prevent the spread of viral hemorrhagic septicemia (VHS) and other fish diseases into the inland waters of New York. For more information visit the Division of Environmental Conservation (DEC) website, www.dec.ny.gov.

INVASIVE SPECIES

While many introduced species have great recreational value, such as Brown Trout, many exotic species have caused problems. Never move fish, water or vegetation from one lake or stream to another, and always follow state laws. Details are available at the DEC website.

FUN WITH FISH

There are many ways to enjoy New York's fish, from reading about them in this book to watching them in the wild. Hands-on activities are also popular. Many resident and nonresident anglers enjoy pursuing New York's game fish. The sport offers a great chance to enjoy the outdoors with friends and family, and in many cases, bring home a healthy meal of fresh fish.

Proceeds from license sales, along with special taxes anglers pay on fishing supplies and motorboat fuel, fund the majority of fish management efforts, including fish surveys, the development of special regulations and stocking programs. The sport also has a huge impact on

New York's economy, supporting thousands of jobs in fishing, tourism and related industries.

CATCH-AND-RELEASE FISHING

Selective harvest (keeping some fish to eat and releasing the rest) and total catch-and-release fishing allow anglers to enjoy the sport without harming the resource. Catch-and-release is especially important with certain species and sizes of fish, and in lakes or rivers where biologists are trying to improve the fishery by protecting large predators or breeding age, adult fish. The fishing regulations, DEC website and your local fisheries' office are excellent sources of advice on which fish to keep and which to release.

Catch-and-release is only truly successful if the fish survives the experience. Following are helpful tips to help reduce the chances of post-release mortality.

- Play and land fish quickly.
- Wet your hands before touching a fish, to avoid removing its protective slime coating.
- Handle the fish gently and keep it in the water if possible.
- Do not hold the fish by the eye sockets or gills. Hold it horizontally and support its belly.
- If a fish is deeply hooked, cut the line so at least an inch hangs outside the mouth. This helps the hook lie flush when the fish takes in food.
- Circle hooks may help reduce deeply hooked fish.
- Don't fish deep water unless you plan to keep your catch.

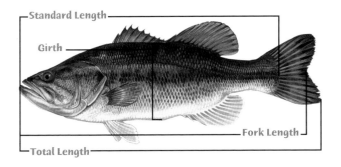

FISH MEASUREMENT

Fish are measured in three ways: standard length, fork length and total length. The first two are more accurate, because tails are often damaged or worn down. Total length is used in slot limits.

The following formulas estimate the weight of popular game fish. Lengths are in inches; weight is in pounds.

Formulas

Bass weight = (length x length x girth) / 1,200
Pike weight = (length x length x length) / 3,500
Sunfish weight = (length x length x length) / 1,200
Trout weight = (length x girth x girth) / 800
Walleye weight = (length x length x length) / 2,700

For example, let's say that you catch a 16-inch Walleye. Using the formula for Walleyes above: (16 x 16 x 16) divided by 2,700 = 1.5 pounds. Your Walleye would weigh approximately 1.5 pounds.

NEW YORK STATE RECORD FISH

SPECIES	WEIGHT (LBS.-OZ.)	WHERE CAUGHT	YEAR
Bass, Hybrid Striped	15-5	Lake Waccabuc, Westchester Co.	2004
Bass, Largemouth	11-4	Buckhorn Lake, Otsego Co.	1987
Bass, Rock	1-15	Ramapo River, Rockland Co.	1984
Bass, Smallmouth	8-4	Lake Erie, Chautauqua Co.	1995
Bass, Striped	55-6	Hudson River, Ulster Co.	2007
Bass, White	3-6	Furnace Brook, Westchester Co.	1992
Bluegill	2-8	Kohlbach Pond, Broome Co.	1992
Bowfin	12-13	Basha Kill, Sullivan Co.	2000
Bullhead, Black	7-7	Mill Pond, Nassau Co.	1993
Bullhead, Brown	6-9	Sugarloaf Pond, Saratoga Co.	1998
Burbot	16-12	Lake Ontario (Black River Bay), Jefferson Co.	1991
Carp, Common	50-4	Tomhannock Reservoir, Rensselaer Co.	1995
Catfish, Channel	32-12	Brant Lake, Warren Co.	2002
Catfish, White	10-5	New Croton Reservoir, Westchester Co.	1998
Cisco (Lake Herring)	5-7	Lake Lauderdale, Washington Co.	1990
Crappie, Black	3-12	Duck Lake, Cayuga Co.	1998
Crappie, White	3-13	Sleepy Hollow Lake, Greene Co.	2001
Drum, Freshwater	24-8	Lake Ontario (Chaumont Bay), Jefferson Co.	2005
Eel, American	7-14	Cayuga Lake, Seneca Co.	1984
Fallfish	3-7	Tioughnioga River, Cortland Co.	2004
Gar, Longnose	13-3	Lake Champlain, Washington Co.	1999
Muskellunge	69-15	St. Lawrence River, Jefferson Co.	1957
Muskellunge, Tiger	35-8	Tioughnioga River, Broome Co.	1990
Perch, White	3-1	Lake Oscaletta, Westchester Co.	1991
Perch, Yellow	3-8	Lake Erie, Erie Co.	1982
Pickerel, Chain	8-1	Toronto Reservoir, Sullivan Co.	1965
Pickerel, Redfin	2-1	Lake Champlain, Essex Co.	1989
Pike, Northern	46-2	Great Sacandaga Lake, Fulton Co.	1940
Pumpkinseed	1-9	Indian Lake, Hamilton Co.	1994
Redhorse, Shorthead	11-11	Salmon River, Oswego Co.	1996
Salmon, Atlantic	24-15	Lake Ontario, Wayne Co.	1997
Salmon, Chinook	47-13	Salmon River, Oswego Co.	1991
Salmon, Coho	33-7	Lake Ontario, Oswego Co.	1998
Salmon, Kokanee	3-6	Boy Scouts Clear Pond, Franklin Co.	2002

SPECIES	WEIGHT (LBS.-OZ.)	WHERE CAUGHT	YEAR
Salmon, Pink	4-15	Lake Erie, Erie Co.	1985
Sauger	4-8	Lower Niagara River, Niagara Co.	1990
Shad, American	9-4	Hudson River, Albany Co.	2007
Splake	13-8	Limekiln Lake, Herkimer Co.	2004
Sucker, White	5-3	Hudson River, Warren Co.	1994
Trout, Brook	4-15	Five Ponds Wilderness Area, Herkimer Co.	2006
Trout, Brown	33-2	Lake Ontario, Oswego Co.	1997
Trout, Lake	41-8	Lake Erie, Chautauqua Co.	2003
Trout, Rainbow	31-3	Lake Ontario, Niagara Co.	2004
Walleye	16-7	Kinzua Reservoir, Cattaraugus Co.	1994
Whitefish, Lake	10-8	Lake Pleasant, Hamilton Co.	1995

FISH CONSUMPTION ADVISORIES

Most fish are safe to eat, but pollutants in the food chain are a valid concern. The DEC routinely monitors contaminant levels in fish and wildlife, and the state Department of Health (DOH) issues an advisory on eating sportfish and wildlife taken in New York State because some of these foods contain potentially harmful levels of chemical contaminants. Advisory information can be found on the DEC website, www.dec.ny.gov, or by calling (518) 402-8924.

These pages explain how the information is presented for each fish.

SAMPLE FISH ILLUSTRATION

Description: brief summary of physical characteristics to help you identify the fish, such as coloration and markings, body shape, fin size and placement

Similar Species: list of other fish that look similar and the pages on which they can be found; includes detailed inset drawings (below) highlighting key physical traits such as markings, mouth size or shape and fin characteristics to help you distinguish this fish from similar species

Brook Trout	**Brown Trout**	**Rainbow Trout**	**Lake Trout**
worm-like marks, red spots	large dark spots, small red dots	pink stripe on silver body	sides lack red spots

SAMPLE COMPARE ILLUSTRATIONS

COMMON NAME
Scientific Name

Other Names: common terms or nicknames you may hear to describe this species

Habitat: environment where the fish is found (such as streams, rivers, small or large lakes, fast-flowing or still water, in or around vegetation, near shore, in clear water)

Range: geographic distribution, starting with the fish's overall range, followed by state-specific information

Food: what the fish eats most of the time (such as crustaceans, insects, fish, plankton)

Reproduction: timing of and behavior during the spawning period (such as dates and water temperatures, migration information, preferred spawning habitat, type of nest if applicable, colonial or solitary nester, parental care for eggs or fry)

Average Size: average length or range of length, average weight or range of weight

Records: state—the state record for this species, location and year; North American—the North American record for this species, location and year (from the National Fresh Water Fishing Hall of Fame)

Notes: interesting natural history information; this can be unique behaviors, remarkable features, sporting and table quality, or details on annual migrations, seasonal patterns or population trends

Description: brownish green back and sides with white belly; long, stout body; rounded tail; continuous dorsal fin; bony plates covering head; males have a large "eye" spot at the base of the tail

Similar Species: American Eel (pg. 42), Burbot (pg. 38), Sea Lamprey (pg. 58)

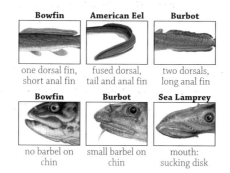

Bowfin	American Eel	Burbot
one dorsal fin, short anal fin	fused dorsal, tail and anal fin	two dorsals, long anal fin

Bowfin	Burbot	Sea Lamprey
no barbel on chin	small barbel on chin	mouth: sucking disk

BOWFIN

Amia calva

Amiidae

Other Names: dogfish, grindle, mudfish, cypress trout, lake lawyer, beaverfish

Habitat: deep waters associated with vegetation in warm water lakes and rivers; feeds in shallow weed beds

Range: Mississippi River drainage east through the St. Lawrence drainage, south from Texas to Florida; found throughout New York but most common in the Great Lakes, Champlain and Finger Lakes, St. Lawrence and lower Seneca Rivers

Food: fish, crayfish

Reproduction: in spring when water exceeds 61 degrees F, male removes vegetation to build a 2-foot nest in sand or gravel; one or more females deposit up to 5,000 eggs in nest; male tenaciously guards the nest and "ball" of young

Average Size: 12 to 24 inches, 2 to 5 pounds

Records: state—12 pounds, 13 ounces, Basha Kill, Sullivan County, 2000; North American—21 pounds, 8 ounces, Forest Lake, South Carolina, 1980

Notes: A voracious predator, the Bowfin prowls shallow weedbeds preying on anything that moves. Once thought detrimental to game fish populations it is now considered an asset in controlling rough fish and stunted game fish. An air breather that tolerates low oxygen levels, the Bowfin can survive buried in mud for short periods during droughts. Not commonly fished for or eaten in New York.

Description: black to olive green back; sides yellowish green; belly creamy white to yellow; light bar at base of tail; barbels around mouth, dark at base; adipose fin; no scales; round tail

Similar Species: Brown Bullhead (pg. 28), Madtom/Stonecat (pg. 36), Yellow Bullhead (pg. 30)

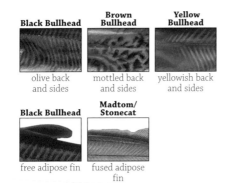

Black Bullhead
olive back and sides

Brown Bullhead
mottled back and sides

Yellow Bullhead
yellowish back and sides

Black Bullhead
free adipose fin

Madtom/Stonecat
fused adipose fin

26

BLACK BULLHEAD

Ameiurus melas

Other Names: common bullhead, horned pout

Habitat: shallow, slow-moving streams and backwaters; lakes and ponds—tolerates extremely turbid (cloudy) conditions

Range: southern Canada through the Great Lakes and the Mississippi River watershed into Mexico and the Southwest; the Erie, Ontario, Genesee and Oswegatchie watersheds in New York

Food: a scavenging opportunist, feeds mostly on animal material (live or dead) but will eat plant matter

Reproduction: spawns from late April to early June; builds nest in shallow water with a muddy bottom; both sexes guard nest, eggs and young to 1 inch in size

Average Size: 8 to 10 inches, 4 to 16 ounces

Records: state—7 pounds, 7 ounces; Mill Pond, Nassau County, 1993; North American—8 pounds, 15 ounces, Sturgis Pond, Michigan, 1987

Notes: The bullhead with most restricted range in New York. It is also the one most tolerant of silt, pollution and low oxygen levels and seems to be increasing in numbers since the 1920s. Young bullheads are black and in early summer are often seen swimming in a tight, swarming ball. Bullheads get little respect but are as tasty as—and much bigger than—most of the panfish taken home to eat.

Description: yellowish brown upper body; mottled back and sides; barbels around mouth; adipose fin; scaleless skin; rounded tail; well-defined barbs on the pectoral spines

Similar Species: Black Bullhead (pg. 26), Madtom/Stonecat (pg. 36), Yellow Bullhead (pg. 30)

Brown Bullhead	Black Bullhead	Yellow Bullhead
mottled back and sides	olive back and sides	yellowish back and sides

Brown Bullhead	Madtom/ Stonecat
free adipose fin	fused adipose fin

28

BROWN BULLHEAD

Ameiurus nebulosus

Other Names: marbled or speckled bullhead, red cat

Habitat: warm, weedy lakes and sluggish streams

Range: southern Canada through the Great Lakes down the eastern states to Florida, introduced in the West; common throughout New York

Food: scavenging opportunist feeding mostly on insects, fish, fish eggs, snails, some plant matter

Reproduction: in early summer males build nest in shallow water vegetation with a sandy or rocky bottom; both sexes guard the eggs and young

Average Size: 8 to 10 inches, 4 ounces to 2 pounds

Records: state—6 pounds, 9 ounces, Sugarloaf Pond, Saratoga County, 1998, (not registered as a North American record); North American—6 pounds, 2 ounces, Pearl River, Mississippi, 1991

Notes: The Brown Bullhead is the most abundant bullhead in New York and can be found in turbid backwaters as well as clear Walleye lakes. It is an important commercial fish in Lake Ontario. The adults are very involved in rearing their young, first by agitating the eggs then guarding the fry until they are about an inch long. Like other catfish, bullheads are nocturnal feeders. Not highly pursued by anglers, though its reddish meat is tasty and fine table fare.

Description: olive head and back; yellowish green head and sides; white belly; barbels on lower jaw are pale green or white; adipose fin; scaleless skin; rounded tail

Similar Species: Black Bullhead (pg. 26), Brown Bullhead (pg. 28), Madtom/Stonecat (pg. 36)

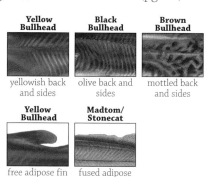

Yellow Bullhead	Black Bullhead	Brown Bullhead
yellowish back and sides	olive back and sides	mottled back and sides

Yellow Bullhead	Madtom/Stonecat
free adipose fin	fused adipose fin

30

YELLOW BULLHEAD

Ameiurus natalis

Other Names: white-whiskered bullhead, yellow cat

Habitat: warm, weedy lakes and sluggish streams

Range: southern Great Lakes through the eastern half of the U.S. to the gulf and into Mexico, introduced in the West; the Allegheny and Great Lakes drainages in western New York, the Hudson River in the east

Food: scavenging opportunist feeding on insects, crayfish, snails, small fish, some plant matter

Reproduction: from late spring to early summer males build nest in shallow water with some vegetation and a soft bottom; both sexes guard the eggs and young

Average Size: 8 to 10 inches, 1 to 2 pounds

Records: state—none; North American—4 pounds, 15 ounces, Ogeechee River, Georgia, 2003

Notes: The Yellow Bullhead is the least tolerant bullhead of turbidity (cloudy water) and is more commonly found in clear streams or ponds. Bullheads feed by "taste" locating food by following chemical trails through the water. This ability can be greatly diminished in polluted water impairing the bullhead's ability to find food. The Yellow Bullhead is less likely than other bullheads to overpopulate a lake and become stunted.

Description: steel gray to silver on the back and sides; white belly; black spots on the sides; large fish lack spots and appear dark olive or slate gray; forked tail; adipose fin; long barbels around mouth

Similar Species: Bullheads (pp. 26-30), White Catfish (pg. 34)

Channel Catfish	Bullheads
deeply forked tail	tail rounded or slightly notched

Channel Catfish	White Catfish
24-30 rays in anal fin, spots	22 to 24 rays in anal fin, no spots

Channel Catfish	White Catfish
spots on side	sides lack spots

CHANNEL CATFISH

Ictalurus punctatus

Other Names: spotted, speckled or silver catfish, fiddler

Habitat: medium to large streams with deep pools, low to moderate current and sand, gravel or rubble bottom; also found in warm lakes; tolerates turbid (cloudy) conditions

Range: southern Canada through the Midwest into Mexico and Florida; widely introduced; native to eastern New York, introduced in warmwater rivers and reservoirs statewide

Food: insects, crustaceans, fish, some plant matter

Reproduction: matures at 2 to 4 years; in summer when water temperature reaches about 70 to 85 degrees F, male builds nest in dark, sheltered area, such as undercut bank; female deposits 2,000 to 21,000 eggs, which hatch in 6 to 10 days; male guards eggs and young until the nest is deserted

Average Size: 12 to 20 inches, 3 to 4 pounds

Records: state—32 pounds, 12 ounces, Brant Lake, 2002; North American—58 pounds, Santee Cooper Reservoir, South Carolina, 1964

Notes: Though not highly respected by many New York anglers, the Channel Catfish can put up a strong fight and is fine table fare. Like other catfish, Channels are nocturnal and are most successfully fished for at night. Channel Catfish were the first widely farmed fish in the U.S. and are now common in grocery stores and restaurants throughout the country.

Description: bluish silver body and off-white belly; older fish dark blue with some mottling; forked tail with pointed lobes; lacks scales; adipose fin; white chin barbels

Similar Species: Channel Catfish (pg. 32)

White Catfish — 22 to 24 rays in anal fin, no spots

Channel Catfish — 24 to 30 rays in anal fin

White Catfish — sides lack spots

Channel Catfish — spots on side

WHITE CATFISH

Ameiurus catus

Other Names: silver or weed catfish, whitey

Habitat: fresh to slightly brackish water of coastal streams; shallow lakes with good vegetation and firm bottom

Range: Maine south to Florida and west to Texas; introduced in some western states; common in much of New York

Food: insects, crayfish, small fish, some plant debris

Reproduction: male builds nest in sheltered areas with a sand or gravel bottom when water temperatures reach the high 60s F, both sexes guard nest and eggs until fry disperse

Average Size: 10 to 18 inches, 1 to 2 pounds

Records: state—10 pounds, 5 ounces, New Croton Reservoir, Westchester County, 1998; North American—22 pounds, William Land Park Pond, California, 1994

Notes: The White Catfish is an abundant species of the coastal streams and ponds of New York and seems to be intermediate between Channel Catfish and bullheads in habits. White Catfish prefer quieter water than Channel Catfish with a somewhat firmer bottom than that sought by bullheads. They frequent the edge of reed beds and are often caught when still fishing the bottom near deep water. Not thought of as a great sportfish, but they do have firm flesh and fine flavor.

STONECAT

TADPOLE MADTOM

Description: Stonecat—similar but lacks dark stripe, and has protruding upper jaw; Tadpole Madtom—dark olive to brown; dark line on side; large, fleshy head; both species have adipose fin continuous with tail

Similar Species: Bullheads (pp. 26–30), Catfish (pp. 32–34)

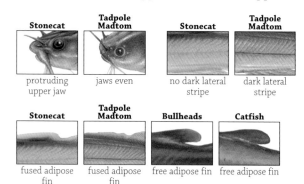

Stonecat	Tadpole Madtom	Stonecat	Tadpole Madtom
protruding upper jaw	jaws even	no dark lateral stripe	dark lateral stripe

Stonecat	Tadpole Madtom	Bullheads	Catfish
fused adipose fin	fused adipose fin	free adipose fin	free adipose fin

STONECAT *Noturus flavus*
TADPOLE MADTOM *Noturus gyrinus*

Other Names: willow cat

Habitat: weedy water near shore in medium to large lakes, under rocks in stream riffles

Range: eastern U.S.; both are widespread in New York

Food: small invertebrates, algae and other plant matter

Reproduction: spawn in late spring; females lay eggs under objects such as roots, rocks, logs or in abandoned crayfish burrows; nest guarded by one parent

Average Size: Stonecat—4 to 6 inches; Tadpole Madtom—3 to 4 inches;

Records: none

Notes: Small, secretive fish most active at night. Both species have poison glands under the skin at the base of the dorsal and pectoral fins. Though not lethal, the poison produces a painful burning sensation, reputed to bring even the hardiest anglers to their knees. Stonecats, and to a lesser extent madtoms, are common baitfish in some areas. Reportedly, damaging the "slime" coating (by rolling them in sand) to make handling easier will reduce their effectiveness as bait.

Description: mottled brown with creamy chin and belly; eel-like body, small barbel at each nostril opening; longer barbel on chin; long dorsal fin similar in shape to, and just above, anal fin

Similar Species: American Eel (pg. 42), Bowfin (pg. 24), Sea Lamprey (pg. 58)

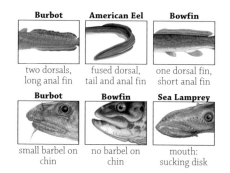

Burbot	American Eel	Bowfin
two dorsals, long anal fin	fused dorsal, tail and anal fin	one dorsal fin, short anal fin

Burbot	Bowfin	Sea Lamprey
small barbel on chin	no barbel on chin	mouth: sucking disk

BURBOT
Lota lota

Other Names: lawyer, eelpout, ling, cusk

Habitat: deep, cold, clear lakes and streams of the north

Range: northern North America into Siberia and across northern Europe; throughout New York except the Delaware, Hudson and Long Island watersheds

Food: a voracious predator; primarily feeds on small fish, but will attempt to eat almost anything including fish eggs, clams and crayfish

Reproduction: pairs to large groups spawn together in mid- to late winter under the ice over a sand or gravel bottom in less than 15 feet of water; after spawning thrashing adults scatter fertilized eggs; no nest is built and no parental care

Average Size: 20 inches, 2 to 8 pounds

Records: state—16 pounds, 12 ounces, Lake Ontario, Jefferson County, 1991; North American—22 pounds, 28 ounces, Little Athapapuskow Lake, Manitoba, 1994

Notes: Burbots are coldwater fish, seldom found in fisheries where the water temperature routinely exceeds 69 degrees F. It is popular with ice fishermen in some western states and Scandinavia but not highly regarded in New York, despite its firm, white, good-tasting flesh.

Description: gray back with purple or bronze reflections; silver sides; white underbelly; humped back; dorsal fin extends from hump to near tail; lateral line runs from head through tail

Similar Species: White Bass (pg. 170)

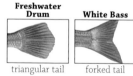

triangular tail   forked tail

down-turned mouth   lower jaw protrudes beyond snout

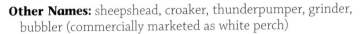

FRESHWATER DRUM

Aplodinotus grunniens

Other Names: sheepshead, croaker, thunderpumper, grinder, bubbler (commercially marketed as white perch)

Habitat: slow- to moderate-current areas of rivers and streams; shallow lakes with soft bottoms, prefers turbid (cloudy) water

Range: Canada south through Midwest into eastern Mexico to Guatemala; in New York the Great Lakes, Oswego and Champlain watersheds

Food: small fish, insects, crayfish, clams, mussels

Reproduction: in May and June after water temperatures reach about 66 degrees F, schools of drum lay eggs near the surface in open water over sand or gravel; no parental care of fry

Average Size: 10 to 14 inches, 2 to 5 pounds

Records: state—24 pounds, 8 ounces, Lake Ontario, Jefferson County, 2005; North American—54 pounds, 8 ounces, Nickajack Lake, Tennessee, 1972

Notes: The only freshwater member of a large family of marine fish. Named for a grunting noise that is made by males, primarily to attract females, but occasionally is made when removed from the water and handled. The sound is produced by specialized muscles rubbed along the swim bladder. The skull contains two enlarged L-shaped earstones called otoliths, once prized for jewelry by Native Americans. The flesh is flaky white and tasty but easily dries out when cooked due to the low oil content.

41

Description: dark brown on top with yellow sides and white belly; long, snake-like body with large mouth; pectoral fins; gill slits; continuous dorsal, tail and anal fin

Similar Species: Bowfin (pg. 24), Burbot (pg. 38), Sea Lamprey (pg. 58)

American Eel

fused dorsal, tail and anal fin

Bowfin

one dorsal fin, short anal fin

Burbot

two dorsals, long anal fin

American Eel

mouth: jaws

Sea Lamprey

mouth: sucking disk

AMERICAN EEL

Anguilla rostrata

Other Names: common, Boston, Atlantic or freshwater eel

Habitat: soft bottoms of medium to large streams, brackish tidewater areas

Range: Atlantic Ocean, eastern and central North America and eastern Central America; all drainages in New York

Food: insects, crayfish, small fish

Reproduction: a "catadromous" species spending most of its life in freshwater returning to the Sargasso Sea in the North Atlantic Ocean to spawn; females lay up to 20 million eggs; adults die after spawning

Average Size: 24 to 36 inches, 1 to 3 pounds

Records: state—7 pounds, 14 ounces, Cayuga Lake, Seneca County, 1984; North American—8 pounds, 8 ounces, Cliff Pond, Massachusetts, 1992

Notes: Leaf-shaped larval eels drift with ocean currents for about a year. When they reach river mouths of North and Central America they morph into small eels (elvers). Males remain in the estuaries; females migrate upstream. At maturity (up to 20 years of age) adults return to the Sargasso Sea. Once commercially harvested, now sought only by anglers for sport and food. Smoked eels have an excellent flavor.

Description: olive to brown with dark spots along sides; long, cylindrical profile; single dorsal fin located just above the anal fin; body encased in hard, plate-like scales; snout twice as long as head; needle-sharp teeth on both jaws

Similar Species: none

LONGNOSE GAR
Lepisosteus osseus

Other Names: garfish

Habitat: quiet water of larger rivers and lakes

Range: central U.S. throughout the Mississippi drainage south into Mexico, a few rivers in the northeast Great Lakes drainages; in New York, lakes Erie, Ontario, Champlain and Chautauqua, and the Oswego, the Seneca and Niagara rivers

Food: minnows and other small fish

Reproduction: large, green eggs are deposited in weedy shallows when water temperatures reach the high 60s F; using a small disc on the snout, newly hatched gar attach to something solid until their digestive tracts develop enough to allow feeding

Average Size: 14 to 24 inches, 2 to 4 pounds

Records: state—13 pounds, 3 ounces, Lake Champlain, Washington County, 1999; North American—50 pounds, 5 ounces, Trinity River, Texas, 1954

Notes: Gars belong to a prehistoric family of fish that can breath air with the aid of a modified swim bladder. This adaptation makes them well suited to survive in the increasingly polluted, slow-moving rivers and lakes. Gars are a valuable asset in controlling growing populations of rough fish in these waters. They hunt by floating motionless, then making a quick, sideways slash to capture prey.

45

Description: dark gray body with black or brown blotches; divided dorsal fin with green border; black spot at base of front dorsal fin; pelvic fin fused to form sucker-like disk; large head with rapidly tapering body

Similar Species: Mottled Sculpin (pg. 124)

Round Goby

straight-edged anal fin; scales

Mottled Sculpin

distinctly scalloped anal fin; lacks scales

ROUND GOBY

Neogobius melanostomus

Other Names: ship or tank goby

Habitat: bottom dweller, favors rocky or weedy shorelines in large, clear lakes, and deep water during the winter

Range: native to the Black and Caspian seas; lakes Erie and Ontario in New York

Food: small fish, crustaceans, fish eggs

Reproduction: long spawning season runs from late spring through early summer; males spread a sticky substance on the undersides of logs or rocks, on which the females attach eggs; several females may use the same nest; male guards nest and may die after spawning season

Average Size: 4 to 5 inches

Records: none

Notes: An invasive species that was transported from Eurasia in the ballast water of oceangoing ships, the Round Goby is a secretive fish that hides under rocks or buries itself in sand. A voracious feeder and prolific breeder, it is spreading rapidly in the Great Lakes, threatening native species. The only plus to this species is that an adult can consume 30 to 50 Zebra Mussels in a day.

Description: blue to blue-green metallic back; silver sides with faint dark stripes; white belly; purple spot just behind the gill, directly above the pectoral fin; large mouth with protruding lower jaw; sharply pointed scales (scutes) along the ventral midline

Similar Species: American Shad (pg. 52), Blueback Herring (pg. 50), Gizzard Shad (pg. 54)

Alewife	**American Shad**	**Blueback Herring**	**Gizzard Shad**
mouth extends to middle of eye; silver-gray body cavity lining; mouth not below snout	mouth extends to back of eye	black body cavity lining	mouth below snout

ALEWIFE

Alosa pseudoharengus

Other Names: ellwife, sawbelly, golden shad, big-eyed or river herring

Habitat: open water of the Great Lakes and a few inland lakes; coastal waters and streams

Range: Atlantic Ocean from Labrador to the Carolinas, St. Lawrence drainage and the Great Lakes; in New York, lakes Ontario, Erie and some Finger Lakes, a few larger rivers (Hudson, Susquehanna, St. Lawrence) and coastal waters

Food: zooplankton, filamentous algae

Reproduction: in the Great Lakes spawning takes place in open water of bays and along protected shorelines during early summer; coastal alewives make spring runs up rivers when the water warms to 50 degrees F to spawn over sandy bottoms in protected bays

Average Size: landlocked, 4 to 8 inches; marine, 12 to 15 inches

Records: none

Notes: There are two populations of alewives in New York, landlocked and marine. The marine population makes large spring runs but has little sport or commercial value. Alewives were first seen in Lake Ontario in the 1870s and Lake Erie in the 1930s. Later they were stocked into the Finger Lakes. These landlocked alewives are important to sportfishing as they form the forage base for introduced salmon and native Lake Trout in our large inland lakes.

Description: deep, laterally compressed silver body with blue back; one dark spot on the shoulder just behind the gill; saw-tooth edge of sharply pointed scales along the belly (scutes); black lining in body cavity (silver in the Alewife)

Similar Species: Alewife (pg. 48), American Shad (pg. 52), Gizzard Shad (pg. 54)

Blueback Herring	Alewife	American Shad	Gizzard Shad
black body cavity lining; mouth extends to middle of eye; underbite	silver-gray body cavity lining	mouth extends to back of eye	mouth below snout

BLUEBACK HERRING

Alosa aestivalis

Clupeidae

Other Names: glut herring

Habitat: coastal marine most of the year, migrates up rivers and streams to spawn, stocked in some freshwater reservoirs

Range: Atlantic coast from Nova Scotia to the St. Johns River, Florida, and associated spawning rivers; in New York, mainly coastal spawning in river mouths but increasingly recorded in the Great Lakes and Lake Champlain where they may be reproducing

Food: marine plankton feeders

Reproduction: Blueback Herring are "anadromous," migrating to the brackish mouth or up rivers to spawn when water temperatures are near 57 degrees F; extended spawning season lasts 3 months; eggs are deposited in moving water over sand or gravel

Average Size: 10 to 12 inches, 12 ounces

Records: none

Notes: The Blueback Herring is closely related to the Alewife and is sometimes found in mixed schools, though they have different spawning habitats. Bluebacks prefer faster, warmer water and a firmer bottom composition than Alewives. Bluebacks may migrate far upstream or spawn in brackish water. In southern states, such large numbers are seen at stream mouths they are called "glut herring."

Description: silver body and blue-gray back; three or more dark spots on the shoulder; body deep and laterally compressed; large mouth extending to back of eye; saw-tooth edge of sharply pointed scales along the belly (scutes)

Similar Species: Alewife (pg. 48), Blueback Herring (pg. 50), Gizzard Shad (pg. 54)

American Shad	**Alewife**	**Blueback Herring**	**Gizzard Shad**
mouth extends to back of eye; jaws even	mouth extends to middle of eye	mouth extends to middle of eye	mouth below snout

AMERICAN SHAD

Alosa sapidissima

Other Names: river, silver or white shad

Habitat: coastal marine most of the year, migrating up large rivers to spawn; landlocked in a few areas

Range: Atlantic coast and associated spawning rivers from Newfoundland to Florida, introduced and established on the Pacific coast; in New York, the Hudson River and a few smaller free-flowing rivers

Food: plankton, crustaceans, small fish

Reproduction: American Shad migrate up spawning rivers when water temperatures reach 62 to 67 degrees F; spawning takes place at night in the large rivers at the mouth of tributary streams; in the north, adults return to sea after spawning; in southern states they often die after spawning

Average Size: 18 to 20 inches, 2 to 3 pounds

Records: state—9 pounds, 4 ounces, Hudson River, Albany County, 2007; North American—11 pounds, 4 ounces, Connecticut River, Massachusetts, 1986

Notes: The American Shad is the largest shad found in New York. The spring run is credited with helping save George Washington's starving troops at Valley Forge and is still an important sportfishing event. There is a small commercial shad harvest on the Hudson River. Creating "fishways" around dams is essential to ensuring shad reproduction.

Description: deep, laterally compressed body; silvery blue back with white sides and belly; young fish have a dark spot on shoulder behind gill; small mouth; last rays of dorsal fin form long thread

Similar Species: Alewife (pg. 48), American Shad (pg. 52), Blueback Herring (pg. 50)

mouth below
snout

mouth not
below snout

jaws even

underbite

Gizzard Shad   **Alewife**   **American Shad**   **Blueback Herring**

GIZZARD SHAD
Dorosoma cepedianum

Other Names: hickory, mud or jack shad

Habitat: large rivers, reservoirs, lakes, swamps and temporarily flooded pools; brackish and saline waters in coastal areas

Range: St. Lawrence and Great Lakes, Mississippi, Atlantic and Gulf Slope drainages from Quebec to Mexico, south to central Florida; in New York, the Great Lakes and larger lakes and rivers

Food: herbivorous filter feeder

Reproduction: spawning takes place in tributary streams and along lakeshores in early summer; schooling adults release eggs in open water without regard to mates

Average Size: 6 to 8 inches, 1 to 8 ounces

Records: state—none; North American—4 pounds, 12 ounces, Lake Oahe, South Dakota, 2006

Notes: The Gizzard Shad is a widespread, prolific fish that is best known as forage for popular game fish. At times it can become over abundant and experience large die-offs. The name "gizzard" refers to this shad's long, convoluted intestine that is often packed with sand. Though Gizzard Shad are a management problem at times, they form a valuable link in turning plankton into usable forage for larger game fish. Occasionally larger Gizzard Shad are caught with hook and line, but they have little food value.

AMERICAN BROOK LAMPREY

Description: eel-like body; round, sucking-disk mouth; seven paired gill openings; dorsal fin long, extending to tail; no paired fins

Similar Species: American Eel (pg. 42), Bowfin (pg. 24), Burbot (pg. 38), Sea Lamprey (pg. 58)

Native Lampreys	American Eel	Bowfin	Burbot
mouth is a sucking disk	mouth has jaws	mouth has jaws	mouth has jaws

Native Lampreys	Sea Lamprey
undivided dorsal fin	dorsal divided by deep notch

56

NATIVE LAMPREYS

Ichthyomyzon, Lampetra

Species Names: Ohio Lamprey, Silver Lamprey, American Brook, Mountain Brook, and Northern Brook Lampreys

Habitat: juveniles live in the quiet pools of streams and rivers; some adults may move into lakes

Range: fresh waters of eastern North America; Ohio Lamprey in the Ohio drainage to the Alleghenies; Northern Brook Lamprey in western and northern New York; Mountain Brook Lamprey in the Allegheny River drainage; Silver Lamprey in tributaries of lakes Erie, Ontario and Champlain and the St. Lawrence and Hudson rivers; American Brook Lamprey widespread throughout the state

Food: juvenile lampreys are bottom filter feeders in streams, adults are either parasitic on fish or do not feed

Reproduction: adult build nest in gravel of streambeds when water reaches mid 50s F; adults die after spawning

Average Size: 6 to 12 inches

Records: none

Notes: Lampreys are primitive fish with skeletons made of cartilage. As adults Ohio and Silver Lampreys are parasitic often leaving small round wounds on their prey. The three Brook lampreys are not parasitic and adults do not feed. All native lampreys coexist with other New York fish with little or no effect on their populations. Due to deteriorating water conditions, many native lampreys are endangered or threatened throughout their range.

Description: eel-like body; round, sucking-disk mouth; seven paired gill openings; long dorsal fin extends to tail and is divided into two parts by a deep notch; no paired fins

Similar Species: American Eel (pg. 42), Bowfin (pg. 24), Burbot (pg. 38), Native Lampreys (pg. 56)

Sea Lamprey

mouth is a sucking disk

Bowfin

mouth has jaws

Burbot

mouth has jaws

American Eel

mouth has jaws

Sea Lamprey

dorsal fin divided by deep notch

Native Lampreys

undivided dorsal fin

SEA LAMPREY
Petromyzon marinus

Other Names: landlocked or lake lamprey

Habitat: juveniles live in quiet pools of freshwater streams; adults are free-swimming in lakes or oceans

Range: Atlantic Ocean from Greenland to Florida, Norway to the Mediterranean; in New York, they are found in lakes Ontario, Erie, Seneca, Cayuga, Champlain and Oneida, and in coastal streams and rivers

Food: juvenile is a filter feeder in streams; adult is parasitic, attaching to fish with a disk-shaped sucker mouth, then using its sharp tongue to rasp through scales and skin to feed on blood and body fluids; many "host" fish die

Reproduction: adults build nest in the gravel after ascending clear streams, then die shortly after spawning; young remain in the streams several years before returning to the lake or sea as adults

Average Size: 12 to 24 inches

Records: none

Notes: The Sea Lamprey is native to coastal streams of New York and coexists with native species there. With the completion of the Welland Canal, Sea Lampreys entered the Great Lakes with devastating results. Lake Trout and Whitefish fisheries soon collapsed. With the use of traps and chemicals, Canada and New York began controlling lamprey populations in the 1970s and the native fish populations are now recovering.

BIGHEAD CARP

Description: large body; upturned mouth without barbels; low-set eyes; small body scales; no scales on head

Similar Species: Common Carp (pg. 62)

Asian Carp	Common Carp
upturned mouth lacks barbels; eyes low on head	down-turned mouth with barbels

Cyprinidae

ASIAN CARP:

Ctenopharyngodon, Hypophthalmichthys

Species Names: Bighead, Black, Grass and Silver Carp

Habitat: large, warm rivers and connected lakes

Range: native to Asia, introduced in other parts of the world; in New York, Grass Carp are present and established in few streams and ponds; Bighead have been sighted in Lake Erie; Silver and Black, no records to date

Food: Grass Carp—vegetation; Black Carp—mollusks; Silver and Bighead Carp—plankton, mostly algae

Reproduction: spawns from late spring to early summer in warm, flowing water

Average Size: 16 to 22 inches, 5 to 50 pounds

Records: state—none; North American—Bighead Carp, 90 pounds, Kirby Lake, Texas, 2000; Grass Carp, 78 pounds, 12 ounces, Flint River, Georgia, 2003

Notes: Four species of Asian carp were introduced into the United States in southern aquaculture ponds and then escaped to the Mississippi River. Non-breeding (triploid) Grass Carp are permitted in New York for vegetation control and some have escaped. Bighead Carp have been sighted in Lake Erie. The Silver and Black Carp are not known from the state at this time. All four are voracious feeders that have the potential to disrupt the entire food web. The Silver Carp, and to a lesser degree the Bighead Carp, make high leaps from the water when frightened by boats.

Description: brassy yellow to golden brown or dark olive back and sides; white to yellow belly; two pairs of barbels near round, extendable mouth; red-tinged tail and anal fin; each scale has a dark spot at base and a dark margin

Similar Species: Asian Carp (pg. 60)

Common Carp

down-turned mouth with barbels

Asian Carp

upturned mouth lacks barbels; eyes low on head

COMMON CARP

Cyprinus carpio

Cyprinidae

Other Names: German, European, mirror or leather carp, buglemouth

Habitat: warm, shallow, quiet weedy waters of streams and lakes

Range: native to Asia, introduced throughout the world; common throughout New York

Food: opportunistic feeder, prefers insect larvae, crustaceans and mollusks, but will eat algae and some higher plants

Reproduction: spawns from late spring to early summer in very shallow water at stream and lake edges; very obvious when spawning with a great deal of splashing

Average Size: 16 to 18 inches, 5 to 20 pounds

Records: state—50 pounds, 4 ounces, Tomhannock Reservoir, Rensselaer County, 1995; North American—57 pounds, 13 ounces, Tidal Basin, Washington D.C., 1983

Notes: One of the world's most important freshwater species, the fast-growing carp provides sport and food for millions of people throughout its range. This Asian minnow was introduced into Europe in the twelfth century but didn't make it to North America until the 1800s. In New York the first introduction was from fish escaping from a private pond in Newburgh in the early 1830s. Carp are a highly prized sportfish in Europe but have yet to reach that status in the U.S.

Description: dark olive back; iridescent purple or silver sides; white belly; dark spot at base of dorsal fin

Similar Species: Fallfish (pg. 66), Fathead Minnow (pg. 72)

Creek Chub

dark spot at front of dorsal

Fallfish

no dark spot at base of dorsal

Creek Chub

rounded tail

Fallfish

tail sharply pointed

Creek Chub

mouth extends to eye

Fathead Minnow

mouth does not extend to eye

CREEK CHUB

Semotilus atromaculatus

Cyprinidae

Other Names: common, brook, silver, mud or blackspot chub, horned or northern horned dace

Habitat: primarily found in quiet pools in clear streams and rivers, occasionally in lakes

Range: Montana southward through the Gulf States; all New York drainages

Food: small aquatic invertebrates and crustaceans

Reproduction: in late spring, male excavates a 1- to 3-foot-long, teardrop-shaped pit at the head of stream riffles, using its mouth or rolling stones with its head; the pits are filled until 6 to 8 inches high; females lay eggs on the mound, which are then covered and defended by the male; several other minnow species may spawn on the mound, occasionally resulting in hybridization

Average Size: 4 to 10 inches, up to 6 ounces

Records: none

Notes: The Creek Chub is one of the most common stream fishes in eastern North America. They take bait readily and are often fished for by young boys spending a day on the creek. When water levels are low in late summer, the chub spawning mounds can be plentiful and quite evident, leaving many to speculate on their origin. Chubs are a highly prized bait minnow, and local populations can be easily depleted by overharvesting.

Description: black back; dark olive sides; side scales have a black triangular bar on the front corner; large mouth; small barbel fits in a grove between back of upper jaw and snout

Similar Species: Creek Chub (pg. 64), Fathead Minnow (pg. 72)

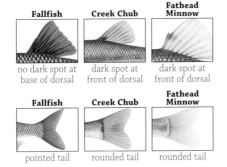

Fallfish	Creek Chub	Fathead Minnow
no dark spot at base of dorsal	dark spot at front of dorsal	dark spot at front of dorsal
Fallfish	**Creek Chub**	**Fathead Minnow**
pointed tail	rounded tail	rounded tail

FALLFISH

Semotilus corporalis

Other Names: windfish, silver chub

Habitat: quiet pools in clear streams and along lake shorelines

Range: Atlantic drainage from New Brunswick to Virginia; all drainages in central New York

Food: small aquatic invertebrates and crustaceans

Reproduction: in late spring, male builds spectacular nest by carrying and rolling stones into a mound that may reach 6 feet long and 3 feet high; several females lay eggs on the mound, which is guarded by the male

Average Size: 10 to 12 inches, 4 to 12 ounces

Records: state—3 pounds, 7 ounces, Tioughnioga River, Cortland County, 2004; North American—3 pounds, 12 ounces, Sibley Pond, Maine, 1986

Notes: The Fallfish is the largest minnow native to New York and is primarily found in the same waters as trout. The larger fish are found in deep pools at the base of rapids; look for smaller ones in the quiet water along the stream edges. Fallfish readily take flies and have a fine flavor, but are not as prestigious as trout.

Description: reddish-olive mottled back and sides; faint dark stripe on sides from head to tail; long, pointy nose; very small scales

Similar Species: Creek Chub (pg. 64), Fathead Minnow (pg. 72), Northern Redbelly Dace (pg. 70)

Longnose Dace	**Fathead Minnow**	**Creek Chub**	**Northern Redbelly Dace**
upper jaw and snout extend well beyond lower jaw	jaws nearly even	upper jaw slightly ahead of lower jaw	lower jaw slightly ahead of upper

LONGNOSE DACE

Rhinichthys cataractae

Other Names: Great Lakes dace, leatherback, stream shooter

Habitat: small and medium-size streams with strong currents; windy, rocky shorelines of large lakes

Range: Northwest Territories to Hudson Bay, northeastern U.S. and eastern Canada; common throughout New York

Food: bottom feeders primarily zooplankton, aquatic insects

Reproduction: spawns in the fast current at the base of riffles when water temperatures reach the low 60s F; males defend a spawning site by butting and biting intruders; a few hundred to a thousand very adhesive eggs are laid, then abandoned

Average Size: 2 to 3 inches

Records: none

Notes: A small group of minnows in New York are referred to as daces. These are small fish that live in a variety of habitats. The Longnose Dace is a strong swimmer that is often found in the active water of fast streams or beach surf. They are hardy fish that can withstand quick environmental changes. Not as colorful as other dace but survives well in cool aquariums.

Description: dark brown to charcoal back; two broad, lateral bands on tan background; in breeding males, tan turns orange and belly becomes bright red or orange; blunt nose

Similar Species: Fathead Minnow (pg. 72), Longnose Dace (pg. 68)

Northern Redbelly Dace	**Fathead Minnow**	**Northern Redbelly Dace**	**Longnose Dace**
prominent lateral bands	lacks prominent lateral bands	lower jaw slightly ahead of upper	upper jaw and snout extend well beyond lower jaw

NORTHERN REDBELLY DACE

Phoxinus eos

Other Names: redbelly, leatherback, yellow-belly dace

Habitat: small streams and bog lakes

Range: Northwest Territories to Hudson Bay, northeastern U.S. and eastern Canada; in New York, the Allegheny, Erie, St. Lawrence, Black and Hudson drainages

Food: bottom feeders, primarily plant material

Reproduction: in early summer a single female attended by several males will dart among masses of filamentous algae, laying 5 to 30 non-adhesive eggs; male fertilizes the eggs, which hatch in 8 to 10 days without parental care

Average Size: 2 to 3 inches

Records: none

Notes: A small group of minnows in New York are referred to as daces. These are small fish that live in a variety of habitats. The Northern Redbelly Dace is a hardy fish that is often found in the acid water of bog lakes and beaver ponds. Redbelly Dace are hardy and withstand low oxygen and crowding well, and were once an important baitfish. Redbelly Dace school when water levels are low, making them susceptible to overharvest. Breeding males are brightly colored and one of New York's most beautiful fish.

NON-SPAWNING ADULT

SPAWNING MALE

Description: olive to slate gray back; dull golden yellow sides; dark side stripe narrows toward tail then widens to dark spot; rounded snout and fins; no scales on head; dark blotch on front of dorsal fin

Similar Species: Creek Chub (pg. 64)

Fathead Minnow	Creek Chub
anal fin has 7 rays	anal fin has 8 rays

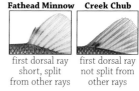

Fathead Minnow	Creek Chub
first dorsal ray short, split from other rays	first dorsal ray not split from other rays

72

FATHEAD MINNOW
Pimephales promelas

Cyprinidae

Other Names: blackhead, tuffy

Habitat: shallow pools of midsize to small streams; shallow, weedy lakes and ponds with few predators

Range: east of the Rocky Mountains in the U.S. and Canada; common throughout New York, except Long Island

Food: primarily algae and other plant matter, also insects and copepods

Reproduction: male prepares nest beneath rocks and sticks; female enters and turns upside down to lay adhesive eggs on overhang; male fans the eggs and massages them with a special mucus-like pad on its back

Average Size: 3 to 4 inches

Records: none

Notes: There are nearly 50 species of minnows found in New York, over 200 known from North America and 1,500 in the world. The carps and goldfish are minnows that were introduced from Asia. Native minnows are small fish ranging from a few inches to a foot long. The Fathead Minnow is one of New York's most numerous and widespread fish. It and the Bluntnose Minnow are common bait minnows and are certainly two of the most economically important fish in the U.S.

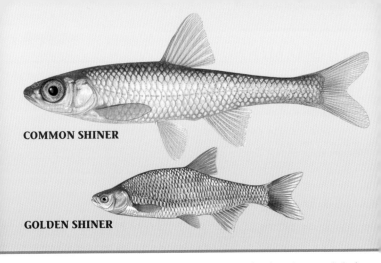

COMMON SHINER

GOLDEN SHINER

Description: silver body with dark green back, often with light body stripe; breeding males have bluish heads and rosy pink body and fins

Similar Species: Creek Chub (pg. 64), Golden Shiner

Common Shiner	Creek Chub
mouth barely extends to eye, which is large in relation to head	mouth extends to middle of eye, which is small in relation to head

Common Shiner	Golden Shiner
usually 9 rays on anal fin	11 to 15 rays on anal fin

COMMON SHINER

Cyprinidae

Luxilus cornutus

Other Names: creek or redfin shiner

Habitat: lakes, rivers and streams; most common in pools of cool, clear streams and small rivers

Range: Midwest through eastern U.S. and Canada; common throughout New York

Food: small aquatic insects, zooplankton, algae

Reproduction: male prepares nest of small stones at the head of stream riffles (sometimes using the nest of Creek or Hornyhead Chubs); male courts females with great flourish and then guards the nest, sometimes in conjunction with Hornyhead Chubs

Average Size: 4 to 12 inches

Records: none

Notes: Almost half the New York minnows are called shiners and most are in the genus *Notropis*. Not all shiners are as flashy as the name indicates; some have dull coloration with almost no silver on the sides. The Common Shiner is a large, showy fish that has now replaced the Golden Shiner as the common bait shiner, though it seems somewhat less hardy on the line. Large Common Shiners can be caught with dry flies and can be very sporting on light tackle but are not meaty enough to put on the table.

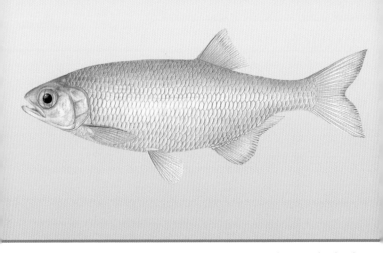

Description: olive back; silver sides; large scales on the body but none on the head; large white eye, over one third width of the head; thin body flattened from side to side with sharp scaleless keel between the pelvic and anal fin; terminal mouth

Similar Species: American Shad (pg. 52), Blueback Herring (pg. 50), Gizzard Shad (pg. 54)

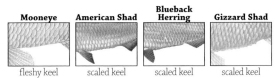

Mooneye	American Shad	Blueback Herring	Gizzard Shad
fleshy keel	scaled keel	scaled keel	scaled keel

MOONEYE

Hiodon tergisus

Other Names: white shad, slicker, toothed herring, river whitefish

Habitat: clear, quiet waters of large lakes and the backwaters of large streams

Range: Hudson Bay drainage east to the St. Lawrence, through the Mississippi drainage south into Arkansas and Alabama; in New York, lakes Ontario, Erie, Champlain and Black, and the St. Lawrence and Oswegatchie rivers

Food: insects, small fish, crayfish, snails

Reproduction: adults migrate up larger tributaries to spawn in early spring when water temperatures reach mid 50s F, eggs with a gelatinous coating are released over gravel bars in fast current

Average Size: 12 inches, 12 to 16 ounces

Records: state—none; North American—1 pound, 12 ounces, Lake Poygan, Wisconsin, 2000

Notes: The Mooneye is a flashy fish that jumps repeatedly when hooked. However, it is bony with little meat except along the back. It feeds on insects near or on the surface in slack waters of large lakes and rivers. Mooneyes look like freshwater herring but are in their own family. They require clean, clear water and are declining over much of their range due to poor water quality. They are a threatened species in New York. Though small, they are related to Arapaima, the world's largest scaled freshwater fish.

Description: olive green back; tan to yellow-brown sides with faint wavy vertical bars; rounded tail fin; dark bar just before the tail; slightly flattened head

Similar Species: Banded Killifish (pg. 178), Fathead Minnow (pg. 72)

Central Mudminnow	**Banded Killifish**		**Central Mudminnow**	**Fathead Minnow**
dark bar or blotch below eye	lacks dark bar or blotch below eye		rounded tail	forked tail

CENTRAL MUDMINNOW

Umbra limi

Other Names: Mississippi or western mudminnow, dogfish, mudfish

Habitat: slow, stagnant waters of weedy streams and ponds with soft bottoms

Range: Great Lakes states through the Midwest; throughout New York except the Delaware and Susquehanna drainages and Long Island

Food: insects, mollusks, larger crustaceans

Reproduction: in the early spring, adults move into flooded pools when water temperatures reach the mid 50s F; yellow-orange eggs are deposited singly on plant leaves and are left to hatch without parental care

Average Size: 3 inches

Records: none

Notes: This hardy little fish can stand very low oxygen levels and gulp air to breathe (even from air bubbles under the ice). They hide in the bottom detritus but do not bury themselves tail first in the mud as often reported. They are frequently the only fish left in ponds after winter die-offs. They are good baitfish, withstanding the bait pail and hook well. They can be fun aquarium fish, quickly learning to eat small pieces of meat or angleworms.

Description: large gray scaleless body; snout protrudes into a large paddle; shark-like forked tail; gills extend into long pointed flaps

Similar Species: Channel Catfish (pg. 32)

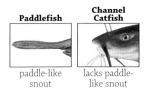

Paddlefish

Channel Catfish

paddle-like snout

lacks paddle-like snout

Polyodontidae

PADDLEFISH

Polyodon spathula

Other Names: spoonbill cat, duckbill

Habitat: deep pools of large rivers and their connecting lakes

Range: large rivers in the Mississippi drainage; Allegheny River in New York

Food: free-swimming plankton

Reproduction: spawning takes place when water levels are rising in the spring and temperatures reach the low 50s F; adults migrate up large tributaries till blocked by dams; breeding schools gather in moving water less than 10 feet deep to release eggs over large gravel bars

Average Size: 2 to 4 feet, 20 to 40 pounds

Records: state—none; North American—144 pounds, Dam No. 7, Kansas, 2004

Notes: This prehistoric fish is very shark-like in anatomy, with its only close relative found in the Yangtze River of China. Paddlefish have a large mouth but no teeth and feed entirely on plankton. The function of the paddle is not well understood but it is not used to dig in the mud. Scientists believe that sensors in the paddle detect electrical currents created by clouds of plankton. The few populations that once existed in the Northeast have been extirpated, but Paddlefish were recently reintroduced into Allegheny Reservoir.

IOWA DARTER

JOHNNY
DARTER

Description: Iowa Darter—brown back with faint blotches; sides have 9 to 10 vertical bars; dark spot under the eye; bars become more pronounced and colors brighter on breeding males; Johnny Darter—tan to olive back and upper sides with dark blotches and speckling; sides tan to golden with X, Y and W patterns; breeding males dark with black bars

Similar Species: Iowa Darter, Johnny Darter

Iowa Darter

blotches or bars
on sides

Johnny Darter

X, Y and W
markings

82

Percidae

IOWA DARTER *Etheostoma exile*
JOHNNY DARTER *Etheostoma nigrum*

Other Names: red-sided, yellowbelly or weed darter

Habitat: Iowa Darters inhabit fast waters of clear streams; Johnny Darters prefer shallow water in lakes that have some vegetation or algae mat

Range: Rocky Mountains east across Canada and the U.S. through the Great Lakes region; both darters are native to western New York

Food: small aquatic invertebrates

Reproduction: in May and June, males migrate to shorelines to establish breeding areas; females move from territory to territory, spawning with several males; each sequence produces 7 to 10 eggs that attach to the bottom

Average Size: 2 to 4 inches

Records: none

Notes: Relatives of Yellow Perch and Walleye, darters are primarily stream fish adapted to living among the rocks in fast current. A small swim bladder allows darters to sink rapidly to the bottom after a "dart," thus avoiding being swept away by the current. Darters are hard to see when they move but are easy to spot when perched on their pectoral fins. The Iowa Darter is primarily a stream species while the Johnny Darter prefers weedy lake shorelines, but both can be found in a large range of habitats.

Description: slender body; gray to dark silver or yellowish brown with dark blotches on sides; black spots on spiny dorsal fin; may exhibit some white on lower margin of tail, but lacks prominent white spot found on Walleye

Similar Species: Walleye (pg. 86)

Sauger	Walleye		Sauger	Walleye
spiny dorsal fin is spotted, lacks dark blotch on rear base	spiny dorsal fin lacks spots, has large dark blotch on rear base		blotches on sides below lateral line	lacks blotches on sides below lateral line

SAUGER

Sander canadensis

Other Names: sand pike, spotfin pike, river pike, jackfish, jack salmon

Habitat: large lakes and rivers

Range: large lakes in southern Canada, northern U.S. and the larger reaches of the Mississippi, Missouri, Ohio and Tennessee River drainages; in New York, the Great Lakes and Oswego drainage, St. Lawrence River and Lake Champlain

Food: small fish, aquatic insects, crayfish

Reproduction: spawns in April and May as water approaches 50 degrees F; adults move into the shallow waters of tributaries and headwaters to randomly deposit eggs over gravel beds

Average Size: 10 to 12 inches, 8 ounces to 2 pounds

Records: state—4 pounds, 8 ounces; Lower Niagara River, Niagara County, 1990; North American—8 pounds, 12 ounces, Lake Sakakawea, North Dakota, 1971

Notes: Though the Sauger is the Walleye's smaller cousin it is a big-water fish residing primarily in large lakes and rivers. It is slow growing, often reaching only two pounds in twenty years. Saugers are an important sportfish summer and winter, particularly in Lake Champlain and the Niagara River. Saugers are aggressive daytime feeders compared to Walleyes, and their fine-flavored flesh is top table fare.

85

Description: long, round body; dark silver or golden to dark olive brown sides; spines in both first dorsal and anal fin; sharp canine teeth; dark spot at base of the three last spines of the dorsal fin; white spot on bottom lobe of tail

Similar Species: Sauger (pg. 84)

Walleye	Sauger	Walleye	Sauger
spiny dorsal fin lacks spots, has large dark blotch on rear base	spiny dorsal fin is spotted, lacks dark blotch on rear base	lacks blotches on sides below lateral line	blotches on sides below lateral line

WALLEYE
Sander vitreus

Other Names: marble-eyes, walleyed pike, jack, jackfish, Susquehanna salmon

Habitat: lakes and streams, abundant in very large lakes

Range: originally the northern states and Canada, now widely stocked throughout the U.S.; stocked throughout New York

Food: mainly small fish, also insects, crayfish, leeches

Reproduction: spawns in tributary streams or rocky lake shoals when spring water temperatures reach 45 to 50 degrees F; no parental care

Average Size: 14 to 17 inches, 1 to 3 pounds

Records: state—16 pounds, 7 ounces, Kinzua Reservoir, Cattaraugus County, 1994; North American—22 pounds, 11 ounces, Greer's Ferry Lake, Arkansas, 1982

Notes: The Walleye is a popular sportfish—not a great fighter, but a dogged opponent and fine eating fish. A reflective layer of pigment in the eye allows the Walleye to see in low light conditions, thus Walleyes are most active under cloudy skies, at dusk and dawn and through the night. The Blue Pike, a subspecies (*S. vitreum glaucum*) of the Walleye, was once very common in Lake Erie but is now thought to be extinct.

Description: 6 to 9 olive-green vertical bars on a yellow-brown background; two separate dorsal fins, the front all spines, the back soft rays; lower fins tinged yellow or orange, brighter in breeding males

Similar Species: Trout-perch (pg. 180), Walleye (pg. 86)

Yellow Perch	**Trout-perch**	**Yellow Perch**	**Walleye**
lacks adipose fin	adipose fin	lacks large white spot on tail	large white spot on tail

YELLOW PERCH
Perca flavescens

Other Names: ringed, striped or jack perch, green hornet

Habitat: lakes and streams, prefers clear, open water

Range: widely introduced throughout southern Canada and northern U.S.; common throughout New York

Food: prefers minnows, insects, snails, leeches and crayfish

Reproduction: spawns at night in shallow weedy areas when water temperatures reach 45 degrees F; female drapes gelatinous ribbons of eggs on submerged vegetation

Average Size: 8 to 11 inches, 6 to 10 ounces

Records: state—3 pounds, 8 ounces, Lake Erie, Erie County, 1982; North American—4 pounds, 3 ounces, Bordentown, New Jersey, 1865

Notes: Yellow Perch are very common in New York and possibly the most important food and sportfish in the state. Perch congregate in large schools and are active throughout the year, providing endless hours of enjoyment for anglers. Yellow Perch reproduction in the Great Lakes seems to be adversely affected by high Alewife populations. However, perch numbers quickly recover in years that the Alewife population crashes.

Description: olive green to yellow-brown back and sides; yellow-green chain-like markings on the sides; distinct dark teardrop below the eye; scales on the entire cheek and gill covers; fins almost clear

Similar Species: Grass Pickerel (pg. 92), Northern Pike (pg. 98), Redfin Pickerel (pg. 94)

Chain Pickerel	Grass Pickerel	Northern Pike	Redfin Pickerel

vertical bar under eye	bar under eye angled backward	no vertical bar under eye	bar under eye angled backward

Chain Pickerel	Grass Pickerel	Redfin Pickerel
chain-like marks on sides	lacks distinct chain marks	lacks distinct chain marks

CHAIN PICKEREL

Esox niger

Other Names: weed pike

Habitat: shallow, weedy lakes and sluggish streams

Range: eastern U.S. from the Great Lakes and Maine to Florida west through Gulf States to Texas; common throughout New York

Food: small fish, aquatic invertebrates

Reproduction: spawning takes place in April and May just as the ice goes out; adhesive eggs are deposited over shallow submerged vegetation and left to hatch with no parental care; occasionally spawns in fall with very low survival rate

Average Size: 15 to 18 inches, 1 to 2 pounds

Records: state—8 pounds, 1 ounce, Toronto Reservoir, Sullivan County, 1965; North American—9 pounds, 6 ounces, Homerville, Georgia, 1961

Notes: The Chain Pickerel is the largest of the pickerels and a respected game fish. It frequents the outside edges of weedbeds and bites readily on minnow-imitating lures. When fished on light tackle or a fly rod, it is a very sporting catch. Has a tendency to stunt when overcrowded, filling a lake with $1/2$-pound "hammer-handles."

Description: olive green to yellow-brown back and sides; yellowish wavy bars on sides; dark teardrop below eye; fins cream to pale yellow; scales on entire cheek and gill covers

Similar Species: Chain Pickerel (pg. 90), Northern Pike (pg. 98), Redfin Pickerel (pg. 94)

Grass Pickerel

bar under eye

Northern Pike

no bar under eye

Grass Pickerel

more than six notched scales between pelvic fins

Redfin Pickerel

up to three notched scales between pelvic fins

Grass Pickerel

lacks distinct chain marks

Chain Pickerel

chain-like marks on sides

Esocidae

GRASS PICKEREL

Esox americanus vermiculatus

Other Names: mud or little pickerel, grass or mud pike

Habitat: shallow, weedy lakes and sluggish streams

Range: eastern one-third of the U.S. from the Great Lakes basin to Maine and south to Florida (west of Alleghenies) west through Gulf States; in New York, the Allegheny, Ontario, Erie and St. Lawrence drainages

Food: small fish, aquatic insects

Reproduction: spawning takes place in April and May just as the ice goes out; adhesive eggs are deposited over shallow, submerged vegetation; eggs are left to hatch with no parental care; similar spawning biology results in occasional hybridization with Chain Pickerel

Average Size: 10 to 12 inches, under 1 pound

Records: state—none; North American—1 pound, Dewart Lake, Indiana, 1990

Notes: The Grass Pickerel and the Redfin Pickerel are varieties of the same species. The Redfin is the Atlantic coastal variety, while the Grass Pickerel is the central U.S. variety. They co-mingle in the Gulf States but are separated by range in New York. Both pickerels inhabit dense aquatic vegetation and though small, are scrappy fighters on light tackle. It is unclear what relationship there is between Grass Pickerel and Northern Pike. In some lakes they coexist; in others there is just one species or the other.

Description: olive green to yellow-brown back and sides; sides have worm-like bars; distinct dark teardrop below eye; lower fins are tinged red, bright red in breeding males; scales on the entire cheek and gill cover

Similar Species: Chain Pickerel (pg. 90), Grass Pickerel (pg. 92), Northern Pike (pg. 98)

Redfin Pickerel / **Northern Pike**

bar under eye / no bar under eye

Redfin Pickerel

up to three notched scales between pelvic fins

Grass Pickerel

more than six notched scales between pelvic fins

Redfin Pickerel / **Chain Pickerel**

lacks distinct chain marks / chain-like marks on sides

REDFIN PICKEREL

Esox americanus americanus

Other Names: little or mud pickerel, red, grass or mud pike

Habitat: shallow, weedy lakes and sluggish streams

Range: Atlantic States from Maine to Florida (east of Alleghenies) and east through the Gulf States; eastern New York in the Hudson, Delaware and Long Island drainages

Food: small fish, aquatic invertebrates

Reproduction: spawns in early spring just as the ice goes out when adults enter flooded meadows and shallow bays to lay eggs in less than 2 feet of water; adhesive eggs are deposited over shallow, submerged vegetation; eggs are left to hatch with no parental care; similar spawning biology results in the occasional hybridization with Chain Pickerel

Average Size: 10 to 12 inches, under 1 pound

Records: state—2 pounds, 1 ounce, Lake Champlain, Essex County, 1989; North American—2 pounds, 10 ounces, Lewis Lake, Georgia, 1982

Notes: The Grass Pickerel and the Redfin Pickerel are varieties of the same species. The Redfin is the Atlantic coastal version; the Grass Pickerel is the central U.S. variety. They co-mingle in the Gulf States but are separated by range in New York. Both inhabit dense aquatic vegetation and though small are scrappy fighters on light tackle. Redfin Pickerel eat some small fish, but their diet is mainly larger invertebrates, including crayfish.

MUSKELLUNGE

TIGER MUSKIE

Description: torpedo-shaped body; dorsal fin near tail; dark gray-green back; silver to silver-green sides; dark vertical bars or blotches on sides (dark markings on light background); pointed tail; no scales on lower half of gill covers

Similar Species: Chain Pickerel (pg. 90), Northern Pike (pg. 98)

Muskellunge	Chain Pickerel	Northern Pike
dark marks on light background	chain-like marks on sides	light marks on dark background

Muskellunge	Northern Pike	Tiger Muskie
pointed tail	rounded tail	rounded tail

MUSKELLUNGE

Esocidae

Esox masquinongy

Other Names: muskie, Great Lakes or Ohio Muskellunge

Habitat: waters of large, clear, weedy lakes; medium to large rivers with slow currents and deep pools

Range: the Great Lakes basin east to Maine, south through the Ohio River drainage to Tennessee; in New York, lakes Erie, Ontario and Champlain, along with the St. Lawrence and Oswegatchie drainages

Food: small fish; occasionally baby muskrats, ducklings

Reproduction: spawning takes place in late spring when water temperatures reach 50 to 60 degrees F; eggs are laid in dead vegetation in streams or bays with a soft bottom

Average Size: 30 to 42 inches, 10 to 20 pounds

Records: Muskellunge state—69 pounds, 15 ounces, St. Lawrence River, Jefferson County; 1957; North American—69 pounds, 11 ounces, Chippewa Flowage, Wisconsin 1949

Notes: The Muskellunge is the prize of freshwater fishing. This big, fast predator prefers large, shallow, clear lakes. Muskies are rare to uncommon over most of their range, typically one fish every two to three acres. They are hard to entice with lures or bait and muskie fishermen average over 50 hours to catch a legal fish. Muskellunge occasionally hybridize with Northern Pike to produce Tiger Muskellunge. Tiger Muskies are now reared and stocked in New York's larger lakes.

Description: elongated body with dorsal fin near tail; head long and flattened in front, forming a duck-like snout; dark green back; light green sides with bean-shaped light spots (light markings on dark background)

Similar Species: Chain Pickerel (pg. 90), Muskellunge (pg. 96), Tiger Muskie (pg. 96)

Northern Pike	Chain Pickerel	Muskellunge	Tiger Muskie
light spots on dark background	chain-like marks on sides	dark marks on light background	dark marks on light background

Northern Pike	Muskellunge
rounded tail	pointed tail

NORTHERN PIKE

Esox lucius

Other Names: northern, pickerel or great northern pickerel, jack or jackfish, hammer-handle, snot rocket

Habitat: lakes and slow-moving streams often associated with vegetation

Range: northern Europe, Asia and North America; native to western New York, now common throughout the state except Delaware, Susquehanna and Long Island drainages

Food: small fish, occasionally frogs, crayfish

Reproduction: in early spring as water temperatures reach 34 to 40 degrees F, eggs are laid among shallow vegetation in tributary streams and lake edges; no parental care

Average Size: 18 to 24 inches, 2 to 5 pounds

Records: state and North American—46 pounds, 2 ounces, Great Sacandaga Lake, Fulton County, New York, 1940

Notes: This large, fast predator is one of the most widespread freshwater fish in the world and a prime sportfish throughout its range. Its long, tube-shaped body and intramuscular bones are adaptations for quick bursts of speed. Pike are sight feeders and hunt by lying in wait, capturing prey with a lightning-fast lunge. Many anglers have lost their catches at the boat when the pike employed this burst of speed to escape. The Tiger Muskie is the Northern Pike-Muskellunge hybrid and is considered a Muskie in bag limits.

Description: back is olive, blue-gray to black with wormlike markings; sides bronze to olive with red spots tinged light brown; lower fins red-orange with white leading edge; tail squared or slightly forked

Similar Species: Brown Trout (pg. 102), Rainbow Trout (pg. 108), Lake Trout (pg. 106), Splake (pg. 106)

Brook Trout	**Brown Trout**	**Rainbow Trout**	**Lake Trout**
worm-like marks, red spots	large dark spots, small red dots	pink stripe on silver body	sides lack red spots

Brook Trout	**Lake Trout**	**Splake**
tail square to slightly forked	tail deeply forked	tail moderately forked

BROOK TROUT

Salvelinus fontinalis

Salmonidae

Other Names: speckled, squaretail or coaster trout, brookie

Habitat: cool, clear streams and small lakes with sand or gravel bottoms and moderate vegetation; prefers water temperatures of 50 to 60 degrees

Range: Great Lakes region north to Labrador, south through the Appalachians to Georgia; introduced into the western U.S., Canada, Europe and South America; common in New York streams

Food: insects, small fish, leeches, crustaceans

Reproduction: spawns in late fall when water temperatures reach 40 to 49 degrees F, on gravel bars in riffles, and in lakes where springs can aerate eggs; female builds 4- to 12-inch-deep nest, then buries fertilized eggs in loose gravel; eggs hatch in 50 to 150 days

Average Size: 8 to 10 inches, 8 ounces

Records: state—4 pounds, 15 ounces, Five Ponds Wilderness Area, Herkimer County, 2006; North American— 14 pounds, 8 ounces, Nipigon River, Ontario, 1916

Notes: The Brook Trout is a beautiful fish native to New York's cold, clear streams and is the state fish. Brook Trout are not very tolerant of environmental change and many New York streams can no longer support stable populations. Brook Trout are routinely stocked throughout New York. The bright orange flesh of brookies is firm and has a delicate flavor prized by trout fishermen.

BROWN TROUT

TIGER TROUT

Description: golden brown to olive back and sides; large dark spots on sides, dorsal fin and sometimes upper lobe of tail; red spots with light halos scattered along sides

Similar Species: Atlantic Salmon (pg. 110), Brook Trout (pg. 100), Lake Trout (pg. 106), Rainbow Trout (pg. 108)

Brown Trout	**Rainbow Trout**	**Lake Trout**	**Brook Trout**
dark spots on brown or olive	pink stripe on silvery body	white spots on dark background	worm-like markings on back

Brown Trout	**Atlantic Salmon**
mouth extends beyond back of eye	mouth extends no farther than back of eye

BROWN TROUT

Salmo trutta

Salmonidae

Other Names: German brown, Loch Leven or spotted trout

Habitat: open ocean near its spawning streams and clear, cold, gravel-bottomed streams; shallow portions of the Great Lakes

Range: native to Europe from the Mediterranean to Arctic Norway and Siberia; introduced worldwide; in New York, found in all suitable streams

Food: insects, crayfish, small fish

Reproduction: spawns October through December in headwater streams, tributaries and stream mouths when migration is blocked; female fans out saucer-shaped nest that male guards until spawning, female covers eggs

Average Size: 11 to 20 inches, 2 to 6 pounds

Records: state—33 pounds, 2 ounces, Lake Ontario, Oswego County, 1997; North American—40 pounds, 4 ounces, Little Red River, Arkansas, 1992

Notes: This European trout was brought to North America in the late 1800s and soon replaced the Brook Trout in many streams. It prefers cold, clear streams but will tolerate much warmer water and some turbidity (cloudy water) better than other trout. A favorite of fly-fishermen due to its secretive, hard-to-catch nature, hard fight and fine, delicate flavor. Brown trout often aggressively feed on cloudy, rainy days and at night. Many states have rules restricting night trout fishing. Brown Trout hybridize with Brook Trout to produce the colorful but sterile Tiger Trout.

103

Description: golden yellow body with a faint red stripe; cheeks shaded red; lower fins pinkish; lacks spots of normal rainbows; adipose fin; Palomino Trout lighter colored than Golden Rainbow Trout

Similar Species: Rainbow Trout (pg. 108)

Golden Rainbow Trout

golden yellow body, faint red stripe

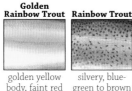

Rainbow Trout

silvery, blue-green to brown body, rose stripe

GOLDEN RAINBOW TROUT

Oncorhynchus mykiss

Other Names: gold trout, goldie

Habitat: prefers whitewater in cool streams and coastal regions of large lakes; tolerates smaller cool, clear lakes

Range: not naturally occurring, stocked in eastern states

Food: insects, small crustaceans, fish

Reproduction: Golden Rainbows are fertile but there is little or no reproduction

Average Size: 15 to 20 inches, 3 to 4 pounds

Records: none; North American—2 pounds, 9 ounces, Beaver Springs, Wisconsin, 1999

Notes: All Golden Rainbow Trout stem from a single female found in a West Virginia hatchery in 1954. The strain was first stocked in New York in the late 1960s but is not currently stocked by the state hatchery system. However, fish from certified private hatcheries may be stocked in select waters with a permit. A Golden Rainbow backcrossed to a normal rainbow gives a Palomino Trout (a much paler Golden Rainbow Trout). Both of these fish show hybrid vigor and grow larger than Rainbow Trout. Palomino Trout are not being stocked at this time. Due to high predation on these brightly colored fish by both anglers and animals, there are few left to reproduce at the end of the summer.

LAKE TROUT

SPLAKE

Description: dark gray to gray-green on the head, back, top fins and tail; white spots on the sides and unpaired fins (light spots on dark background); tail deeply forked; inside of mouth white

Similar Species: Brook Trout (pg. 100), Splake

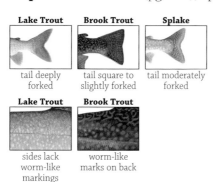

Lake Trout	**Brook Trout**	**Splake**
tail deeply forked	tail square to slightly forked	tail moderately forked

Lake Trout	**Brook Trout**
sides lack worm-like markings	worm-like marks on back

LAKE TROUT

Salvelinus namaycush

Other Names: togue, mackinaw, great gray trout, laker

Habitat: cold (less than 65 degrees F), oxygen-rich waters of deep, clear, infertile lakes

Range: Great Lakes north through Canada, east into northeastern U.S., stocked in the Rocky Mountains; in New York, the Finger Lakes and Erie, Ontario, Champlain, Placid, Blue Mountain, Chazy, George, West Canada, Saranac and Green lakes

Food: insects when very young, small fish to maturity

Reproduction: females scatter eggs over rocky lake bottom when water temperatures dip below 50 degrees F in fall

Average Size: 15 to 20 inches, 7 to 10 pounds

Records: state—41 pounds, 8 ounces, Lake Erie, Chautauqua County, 2003; North American—72 pounds, 4 ounces, Great Bear Lake, N.W.T., Canada, 1995

Notes: The Lake Trout is native to New York and has always been an important part of the Great Lakes fisheries, prized for both food and sport. Lake Trout populations were decimated in the early 1950s by overfishing and the arrival of the Sea Lamprey. With restocking and lamprey control, the population has returned to sportfishing levels. Lake Trout are caught by trolling deep in summer, or "surf" fishing shallower water in spring and fall. Splake is a hybrid trout produced by crossing Brook Trout with Lake Trout.

Description: blue-green to brown head and back; silver lower sides with pink to rose stripe; entire body covered with small black spots; adipose fin

Similar Species: Brook Trout (pg. 100), Brown Trout (pg. 102), Golden Rainbow Trout (pg. 104)

Rainbow Trout

pinkish stripe on silvery body

Brown Trout

sides lack pinkish stripe

Rainbow Trout

silvery, blue-green to brown body, rose stripe

Golden Rainbow Trout

golden-yellow body, faint red stripe

Rainbow Trout

lacks worm-like markings

Brook Trout

worm-like marks on back

RAINBOW TROUT

Oncorhynchus mykiss

Salmonidae

Other Names: steelhead, Pacific, Kamloops or silver trout

Habitat: prefers whitewater in cool streams and coastal regions of large lakes; tolerates smaller, cool, clear lakes

Range: Pacific Ocean and coastal streams from Mexico to Alaska and northeast Russia, introduced worldwide; stocked in New York

Food: insects, small crustaceans, fish

Reproduction: predominantly spring spawners but some fall spawning varieties exist; female builds nest in well-aerated gravel in both streams and lakes

Average Size: streams—10 to 12 inches, 1 pound; lakes—20 to 22 inches, 2 to 3 pounds

Records: state—31 pounds, 3 ounces, Lake Ontario, Niagara County, 2004; North American—(sea-run) 42 pounds, 2 ounces, Bell Island, Alaska, 1970; (inland) 37 pounds, Lake Pend Oreille, Idaho, 1947

Notes: This Pacific trout was brought to New York in 1874 and is common due to continuous stocking. Rainbows are more tolerant of a variety of water conditions than other trout. Some varieties can survive temperatures into the 80s. Steelhead are Rainbow Trout that migrate from spawning streams into the open ocean or lakes for part of their life cycle. An exciting fishery has been created by introducing Steelhead into the Great Lakes. The Niagara River is renowned for its Rainbow Trout fishing.

109

Description: greenish brown back shading to silverish brown sides; light gray belly; black spots on sides; mouth extends no farther than back of eye

Similar Species: Brown Trout (pg. 102)

Atlantic Salmon	Brown Trout
mouth extends no farther than back of eye	mouth extends beyond back of eye

ATLANTIC SALMON
Salmo salar

Other Names: Sebago or Kennebec salmon, ouananiche

Habitat: open ocean and coastal rivers, large clear lakes

Range: historically coastal Atlantic Ocean from Delaware River north to Labrador and across to northern Europe, now stocked in some large U.S. lakes; currently New York stocks a few lakes; few in coastal areas

Food: plankton when young, small fish as adults

Reproduction: both marine and freshwater adults ascend tributary streams in fall to build nests on gravel bars; adults may breed multiple times during their lives; young spend several years in streams before returning to sea

Average Size: 16 to 28 inches, 8 to 10 pounds

Records: state—24 pounds, 15 ounces, Lake Ontario, Wayne County, 1997; North American—(sea-run) 30 pounds, 6 ounces, St. Jean River, Quebec, 1979; (inland) 22 pounds, 11 ounces, Lobstick Lake, Newfoundland, 1924

Notes: Historically there were once both landlocked and sea-run Atlantic Salmon in New York. Lake Ontario and the St. Lawrence River offered one of the greatest salmon fisheries in the world. With overfishing, dam building and pollution Atlantic Salmon all but disappeared from the state. Stocking has returned them to about two dozen waters, including lakes Champlain, Cayuga, Ontario and Seneca.

Description: iridescent green to blue-green back and upper sides, silver below lateral line; small black spots on back and tail; inside of mouth dark; breeding males olive brown to purple with pronounced kype (hooked snout)

Similar Species: Coho Salmon (pg. 114), Kokanee Salmon (pg. 116), Pink Salmon (pg. 118), Rainbow Trout (pg. 108)

Chinook Salmon	**Coho Salmon**	**Kokanee Salmon**	**Pink Salmon**
small spots throughout tail	spots only in top half of tail	tail lacks spots	eye-sized spots throughout tail

Chinook Salmon	**Coho Salmon**	**Rainbow Trout**
inside of mouth is dark	inside of mouth is gray	inside of mouth is white

Salmonidae

CHINOOK SALMON
Oncorhynchus tshawytscha

Other Names: king, spring salmon, tyee, quinnat, black mouth

Habitat: open ocean and large, clear, gravel-bottomed rivers, open waters of the Great Lakes and spawning streams

Range: Pacific Ocean north from California to Japan, introduced to the Atlantic coast in Maine; in New York, lakes Ontario and Erie, mouths of larger tributary streams and the Niagara River

Food: insects, small fish, crustaceans

Reproduction: chinooks in the Great Lakes mature in 3 to 5 years; in September and October they migrate upstream to spawn on gravel bars; eggs hatch the next spring; adults die shortly after spawning

Average Size: 24 to 30 inches, 15 to 20 pounds

Records: state—47 pounds, 13 ounces, Salmon River, Oswego County, 1991; North American—(inland) 44 pounds, 14 ounces, Lake Michigan, 1994; (sea-run) 97 pounds, 4 ounces, Kenai River, Alaska, 1989

Notes: Largest member of the salmon family, the chinook may reach over 40 pounds in lakes and much more in the Pacific. Prior to the 1960s many unsuccessful attempts were made to introduce Chinook Salmon into the Great Lakes region. Since 1965 a stable population of hatchery-reared fish have been maintained in lakes Ontario and Erie, creating one of the most important fisheries in the state. A "put-and-take" fish with little or no natural reproduction.

113

Description: dark metallic blue to green back; silver sides and belly; small dark spots on back, sides and upper tail; inside of mouth gray; breeders gray to green head with red to maroon sides; males develop kype (hooked snout)

Similar Species: Atlantic Salmon (pg. 110), Chinook Salmon (pg. 112), Pink Salmon (pg. 118), Rainbow Trout (pg. 108)

Coho Salmon

spots only in
top half of tail

**Atlantic
Salmon**

few to no spots
in tail

Chinook Salmon

small spots
throughout tail

Pink Salmon

eye-sized spots
throughout tail

Coho Salmon

inside of mouth
is gray

Rainbow Trout

inside of
mouth is white

114

COHO SALMON
Oncorhynchus kisutch

Other Names: silver salmon, sea trout, blueback

Habitat: open ocean near clear, gravel-bottomed spawning streams; open Great Lakes waters within 10 miles of shore

Range: Pacific Ocean north from California to Japan, Atlantic coast of U.S., Great Lakes; in New York, lakes Ontario and Erie and the mouth of larger tributary streams, also the Niagara River

Food: insects, small fish (smelt and alewives)

Reproduction: spawns in October and November; adults migrate up streams to build nest on gravel bars; parent fish die shortly after spawning

Average Size: 20 inches, 4 to 5 pounds

Records: state—33 pounds, 7 ounces, Lake Ontario, Oswego County, 1998; North American—(sea-run) 31 pounds, Cowichan Bay, British Columbia, Canada, 1947; (inland) 33 pounds, 4 ounces, Salmon River, New York, 1989

Notes: This Pacific salmon was first stocked in Lake Erie in the 1870s and many attempts to establish cohos were made during the next 100 years. Despite these efforts, cohos still do not reproduce well in any of the Great Lakes and the populations are maintained by stocking. A very strong fighter and excellent table fare, the Coho Salmon is now an important sportfish in New York.

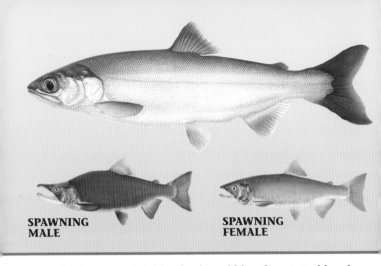

SPAWNING MALE

SPAWNING FEMALE

Description: greenish blue back and bluntly pointed head; silver sides and belly; small black specks on the back and tail; 13 soft rays in anal fin; adipose fin; immature resemble trout; breeding males have bright green heads, red bodies and well-developed kype (hooked snout)

Similar Species: Coho Salmon (pg. 114), Chinook Salmon (pg. 112), Rainbow Trout (pg. 108)

Kokanee Salmon	Coho Salmon	Chinook Salmon	Rainbow Trout
almost toothless; no spots on tail	sharp, medium-size teeth; few spots on tail	small spots throughout tail	many spots on both lobes of tail

Salmonidae

KOKANEE SALMON
Oncorhynchus nerka

Other Names: sockeye or red salmon, silver trout

Habitat: Kokanee—landlocked lakes, Sockeye—open ocean and large, clear, gravel-bottomed rivers

Range: Pacific Ocean north from California to Japan; coastal lakes in northeast North America; introduced elsewhere; in New York, stocked in lakes in the Champlain, Oswegatchie, Black and Hudson drainages

Food: predominately plankton feeders

Reproduction: pairs spawn in fall, usually in tributary streams; female digs bed or "redd" in gravel, sand or rubble; parents guard nest until death, soon after spawning

Average Size: 1 to 3 pounds

Records: state—3 pounds, 6 ounces, Boy Scouts Clear Pond, Franklin County, 2002; North American—9 pounds, 6 ounces, Okanagan Lake, British Columbia, 1988

Notes: The Kokanee Salmon is the landlocked form of the Sockeye Salmon and is stocked in clear lakes in New York. During spawning the males are very distinctive with their hooked beaks and bright colors. Though they primarily eat plankton they can be caught with larger baits or flies and are very popular with anglers.

Description: steel blue to blue-green back with silver sides; dark spots on back and tail, some as large as eye; breeding males form a large hump in front of the dorsal and a hooked upper jaw (kype); both sexes are pink during spawning

Similar Species: Chinook Salmon (pg. 112), Coho Salmon (pg. 114), Kokanee (pg. 116)

Pink Salmon	**Chinook Salmon**	**Coho Salmon**	**Kokanee Salmon**
eye-sized spots throughout tail	small spots throughout tail	spots only in top half of tail	tail lacks predominant spots

Pink Salmon	**Coho Salmon**
dark tongue and jaw tip	inside of mouth is gray

PINK SALMON

Oncorhynchus gorbuscha

Other Names: autumn or humpback salmon, humpy

Habitat: coastal Pacific Ocean and open water of the Great Lakes; spawns in clear streams

Range: coastal Pacific Ocean from northern California to Alaska, Great Lakes; in New York, lakes Ontario and Erie

Food: small fish, crustaceans

Reproduction: spawns in tributary streams usually at two years of age; female builds nest on gravel bars then covers fertilized eggs; adults die after spawning

Average Size: 17 to 19 inches, 1 to 2 pounds

Records: state—4 pounds, 15 ounces, Lake Erie, Erie County, 1985; North American—12 pounds, 9 ounces, Moose and Kenai rivers, Alaska, 1974

Notes: This Pacific salmon was unintentionally released into Lake Superior's Thunder Bay in 1956 and has spread throughout the Great Lakes. Pink Salmon spend two to three years in the open lake then move into streams to spawn and die. In New York there is little or no Pink Salmon reproduction but there are always a few caught by anglers each year. They are not considered good to eat. The flesh deteriorates rapidly and must be quickly put on ice.

Description: silver with faint pink or purple tinge; dark back; light-colored tail; small mouth; long body but deeper than Rainbow Smelt

Similar Species: Lake Whitefish (pg. 122), Mooneye (pg. 76), Rainbow Smelt (pg. 128)

Cisco	Lake Whitefish		Cisco	Mooneye
jaws equal length or slight underbite	snout protrudes beyond lower jaw		adipose fin	lacks adipose fin

Cisco	Rainbow Smelt
deep body (also inconspicuous teeth)	slim profile (also prominent teeth)

CISCO

Coregonus artedi

Other Names: shallow water, common or Great Lakes cisco, lake herring, tullibee

Habitat: shoal waters of the Great Lakes and nutrient-poor inland lakes with oxygen rich depths that remain cool during summer

Range: northeastern U.S., Great Lakes and Canada; in New York, lakes Ontario, Erie, Champlain, Ostego, George, Oneida, Chautauqua and Finger Lakes

Food: plankton, small crustaceans, aquatic insects

Reproduction: spawns in November and December when water temperatures reach the lower 30s F; eggs are deposited over clean bottoms in 3 to 8 feet of water

Average Size: 10 to 12 inches, 1 pound

Records: state—5 pounds, 7 ounces, Lake Lauderdale, Washington County, 1990; North American—7 pounds, 4 ounces, Cedar Lake, Manitoba, 1986

Notes: Ciscoes were once the most productive commercial fish in the Great Lakes. With overfishing, introduced competitors and pollution the population collapsed. Often what is marketed as smoked whitefish are imported Ciscoes. The inland forms of Cisco are known as tullibees and vary greatly in size and shape from one lake to another. Ciscoes can be caught through the ice in winter or by fly-fishermen in summer, particularly when they rise to feed on emerging insects.

Description: silver with a dark brown to olive back and tail; deep body; snout protrudes past lower jaw; small mouth; two small flaps between the openings of each nostril

Similar Species: Cisco (pg. 120), Mooneye (pg. 76), Rainbow Smelt (pg. 128)

Lake Whitefish	**Cisco**
snout protrudes beyond lower jaw	jaws equal length or slight underbite

Lake Whitefish	**Mooneye**
adipose fin	lacks adipose fin

Lake Whitefish	**Rainbow Smelt**
deep body (also inconspicuous teeth)	slim profile (also prominent teeth)

Salmonidae

LAKE WHITEFISH
Coregonus clupeaformis

Other Names: eastern, common or Great Lakes whitefish, Otsego bass, Sault whitefish

Habitat: large, deep, clean inland lakes with oxygen-rich depths during summer; shallow areas of the Great Lakes

Range: from the Great Lakes north across North America; in New York, lakes Ontario, Erie, Champlain, Ostego and Pleasant, introduced into a few other deep, cool lakes

Food: zooplankton, insects, small fish

Reproduction: spawns on gravel bars in late fall when water temperatures reach the low 30s F; occasionally ascends streams to spawn

Average Size: 18 inches, 3 to 4 pounds

Records: state—10 pounds, 8 ounces, Lake Pleasant, Hamilton County, 1995; North American—15 pounds, 6 ounces, Clear Lake, Ontario, 1983

Notes: The largest whitefish in North America and an important food fish from presettlement times to the present. With the control of lampreys and the smelt population collapse, the commercial whitefish harvest has rebounded in the upper Great Lakes. Just before the ice forms in the fall, Lake Whitefish come into the shallows to spawn. A few sportsmen, particularly on Otsego Lake, still fish for whitefish using flies when they are in the shallows, and a jig and cut bait when they are in deep water. Considered by many among the finest food fish from northern waters.

123

Description: slate gray to blotchy olive-brown back; large mouth; eyes set almost on top of head; large, wing-like pectoral fins; no scales

Similar Species: Round Goby (pg. 46)

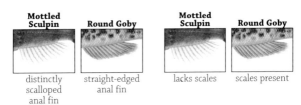

Mottled Sculpin	Round Goby	Mottled Sculpin	Round Goby
distinctly scalloped anal fin	straight-edged anal fin	lacks scales	scales present

MOTTLED SCULPIN

Cottus bairdii

Other Names: common sculpin, muddler, gudgeon

Habitat: bottom-dwellers of cool, swift, hard-bottom streams or wave-swept lakeshores with rocks or vegetation for cover

Range: eastern U.S. through Canada to Hudson Bay and the Rocky Mountains; the Great Lakes, St. Lawrence, Allegheny and Susquehanna drainages in New York

Food: aquatic invertebrates, fish eggs, small fish

Reproduction: spawns in late spring when water temperatures reach 63 to 73 degrees F, male builds nest under ledges, logs or stream banks then entices female with an elaborate courtship; female turns upside down to deposit eggs on "roof" of nest; male attends nest through hatching

Average Size: 4 to 5 inches

Records: none

Notes: A common fish of cool, fast streams that inhabits the same waters as Rainbow and Brown Trout, though it can tolerate somewhat warmer water than trout. To a slight degree sculpins can modify their body color to blend in with the bottom. They are scary looking but perfectly harmless and are forage for many top predators. Sculpins are a preferred bait when fishing for large Brown Trout. Several species of deep-water sculpins native to the Great Lakes are now extinct or nearly so in New York.

Description: long, thin body; sides bright silver to silver-green with conspicuous light stripe; upturned mouth; 2 dorsal fins; tail deeply forked and pointed

Similar Species: Banded Killifish, (pg. 178), Common Shiner (pg. 74)

Brook Silverside	Banded Killifish	Common Shiner
two dorsal fins, long anal fin with straight or concave edge	single dorsal fin, finger shaped anal fin	single dorsal fin, triangular shaped anal fin

BROOK SILVERSIDE
Labidesthes sicculus

Other Names: northern silverside, skipjack, friar

Habitat: surface of clear lakes, slack water of large streams

Range: Great Lakes states south through central U.S. to Gulf states; in New York, the Great Lakes, St. Lawrence, Hudson and Allegheny drainages

Food: aquatic and flying insects, spiders

Reproduction: spawns in late spring and early summer; eggs are laid in sticky strings that are attached to vegetation; most adults die after one spawning

Average Size: 3 to 4 inches

Records: none

Notes: The silverside is in a large family of fish that is mostly tropical and subtropical and primarily marine. It is a flashy fish that is often seen cruising near the lake surface in small schools. Its upturned mouth is an adaptation to surface feeding, and it's not uncommon to see Brook Silversides leap from the water, flying-fish style, in pursuit of prey. Silversides have short life spans lasting only 15 months. There are two marine species of silversides in New York that are restricted to the coast.

Description: dark green back; silver to violet-blue sides; large mouth with prominent teeth; large eye; deeply forked tail; adipose fin

Similar Species: Alewife (pg. 48), Blueback Herring (pg. 50), Gizzard Shad (pg. 54), American Shad (pg. 52)

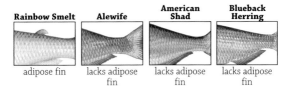

Rainbow Smelt	Alewife	American Shad	Blueback Herring
adipose fin	lacks adipose fin	lacks adipose fin	lacks adipose fin

Gizzard Shad

lacks adipose fin

RAINBOW SMELT

Osmerus mordax

Other Names: ice or frost fish, lake herring, leefish

Habitat: open ocean; cool, medium depths of large lakes; tributary streams for spawning

Range: coastal Pacific, Atlantic and Arctic Oceans, landlocked in southeast Canada and northeast U.S.; in New York, lakes Erie, Ontario, Champlain, Fulton Chain and Finger Lakes, lower Hudson River and spawning streams on Long Island

Food: small crustaceans, insect larvae, small fish

Reproduction: spawns in May at night in the first mile of tributary streams (over bars in open ocean); female lays up to 50,000 eggs that are fertilized by males waiting down-stream; eggs sink, attach to the bottom on short pedestals

Average Size: 8 to 10 inches

Records: none

Notes: Smelt are marine fish that spawn in freshwater. A few northeastern lakes contain native populations. In 1912 fish from Maine were introduced into some Michigan lakes to support the introduced salmon stock. Smelt escaped into Lake Michigan and from there spread to the rest of the Great Lakes (except Ontario, where there is a native population). The Great Lakes smelt population crashed in the 1980s and has not recovered. Smelt are good forage for large predators but consume game fish fry and compete with them for food. Anglers dip net these tasty fish during the spawning run or fish them through the ice.

Description: dark brown back fading to lighter brown sides with irregular blotches; large scales on head; large mouth with sharp teeth; long, single dorsal fin

Similar Species: American Eel (pg. 42), Bowfin (pg. 24), Burbot (pg. 38)

Northern Snakehead	American Eel	Burbot
enlarged scales on head, no barbels	no head scales, bony plates between jaws	barbel on chin

Northern Snakehead	American Eel	Bowfin
long anal fin not fused to tail	short anal fin fused to tail	short anal fin

130

NORTHERN SNAKEHEAD

Channa argus

Other Names: amur or ocellated snakehead, "frankenfish"

Habitat: stagnant shallow ponds and slow-moving streams with mud or weedy bottom

Range: native to China and Korea, introduced to Japan, Eastern Europe and five U.S. states; in New York, Meadow Lake in Queens

Food: fish, crayfish, frogs

Reproduction: females can spawn several times a year beginning in June and lay 100,000 eggs

Average Size: 12 to 24 inches, 2 to 5 pounds

Records: none

Notes: Northern Snakeheads were brought to the U.S. for food in the live fish markets and as aquarium pets, then escaped or were released. The have a modified swim bladder that allows them to breathe air and can slither through wet marshes for up to three days to reach new lakes. Snakeheads are voracious predators that can tolerate temperatures from freezing to near 90 degrees F. This highly competitive invader has the potential to devastate native fish populations. Anglers should learn to identify snakeheads and if any are caught the fish should be killed, frozen and turned over to a conservation officer.

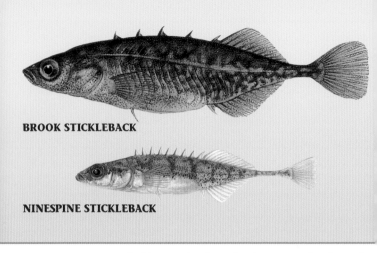

BROOK STICKLEBACK

NINESPINE STICKLEBACK

Description: mottled brown back and sides; torpedo-shaped body with very narrow caudal peduncle (area just before the tail); front portion of dorsal fin has 4 to 6 short, separated spines; pelvic fin (abdominal), reduced to single spine; small, sharp teeth

Similar Species: Ninespine Stickleback

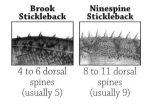

Brook Stickleback	Ninespine Stickleback
4 to 6 dorsal spines (usually 5)	8 to 11 dorsal spines (usually 9)

BROOK STICKLEBACK

Culaea inconstans

Gasterosteidae

Other Names: common or many-spined stickleback, spiny minnow

Habitat: shallows of clear, cool streams and lakes

Range: Kansas through northern U.S. and Canada; freshwater throughout New York

Food: small aquatic animals

Reproduction: males build a golf-ball-size, globular nest of sticks and algae that hangs on submerged vegetation; female enters nest to deposit eggs then departs, often plowing a hole in the side; male repairs nest and viciously guards the eggs until they hatch; male may build a second nest and move eggs

Average Size: 2 to 4 inches

Records: none

Notes: Most members of the stickleback family are marine fish but some are equally at home in fresh- or saltwater, such as the Ninespine Stickleback (*Pungitius pungitius*), which is also found in New York. Highly tolerant of alkaline and acidic conditions but not turbidity (cloudy water), these little fish are becoming rare over much of their range as water conditions deteriorate. Pugnacious little predators, they make fun aquarium fish that will readily build and defend nests in captivity, though they may require live food when first captured (mosquito larvae work well).

Description: slate gray back and sides; five rows of white-tipped bony plates, one on top, two on the sides and two on the bottom; tail is shark-like with the upper lobe much longer than lower; snout is long with a narrow mouth

Similar Species: Lake Sturgeon (pg. 136), Shortnose Sturgeon

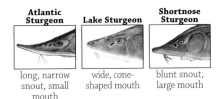

Atlantic Sturgeon	Lake Sturgeon	Shortnose Sturgeon
long, narrow snout, small mouth	wide, cone-shaped mouth	blunt snout, large mouth

ATLANTIC STURGEON

Acipenser oxyrhynchus

Other Names: none

Habitat: large coastal rivers and estuaries

Range: Atlantic coast from Labrador to Florida; Hudson River in New York

Food: snails, clams, crayfish and insects found on the bottom

Reproduction: migrates to brackish estuaries or freshwater rivers to spawn from April through June; many thousands of eggs are laid and fertilized a few at a time; eggs are deposited over gravel bars in the current of large rivers

Average Size: 8 to 12 feet, 300 to 400 pounds

Records: none

Notes: The Atlantic Sturgeon is New York's largest freshwater fish, often 12 to 14 feet long. They spend most of year in the coastal Atlantic then migrate into brackish and freshwater to spawn. They are rare throughout their range and are endangered in most states. The exception is in the Hudson River, where there is a large population estimated at more than 150,000 fish.

Description: dark gray to black back; slate gray to gray-green sides; bony plates on skin; tail shark-like, with upper lobe longer than lower; blunt snout with four barbels; spiracles (openings between eye and corner of gill)

Similar Species: Atlantic Sturgeon (pg. 134), Shortnose Sturgeon

Lake Sturgeon	**Atlantic Sturgeon**	**Shortnose Sturgeon**
wide, cone-shaped mouth	small mouth	prominent white on plates and tail

Lake Sturgeon	**Shortnose Sturgeon**
lacks prominent white on plates and tail	prominent white on plates and tail

136

Acipenseridae

LAKE STURGEON

Acipenser fulvescens

Other Names: rock, stone, red, black or smoothback sturgeon

Habitat: quiet waters in large rivers and lakes

Range: Hudson Bay, Great Lakes, Mississippi and Missouri drainages southeast to Alabama; larger lakes and rivers of New York including lakes Erie, Ontario, Cayuga and Champlain and St. Lawrence River

Food: snails, clams, crayfish, aquatic insects

Reproduction: spawns from April through June in lake shallows and tributary streams; up to a million eggs are laid and fertilized a few at a time

Average Size: 3 to 5 feet, 5 to 40 pounds

Records: state—none; North American—168 pounds, Nattawasaga Lake, Ontario, 1982

Notes: Sturgeons are the most primitive bony fish alive today, with relatives dating back more than 350 million years. They are bottom feeders that require clear, clean, deep lakes or river pools. They mature slowly and do not spawn until 10 to 20 years of age. Lake Sturgeons over 300 pounds and 100 years old have been caught in southern Canada. Once fished commercially in the Great Lakes and St. Lawrence River, they are now threatened throughout much of their range. Not thought of as a sportfish in New York, they are fished for in other Great Lakes states such as Minnesota and Wisconsin.

Description: bright silver back and sides, often with yellow tinge; fins clear; deep body with round blunt head; leading edge of dorsal fin extends into a large, arching "quill"

Similar Species: Common Carp (pg. 62)

Quillback   **Common Carp**

mouth lacks   barbels below
barbels   mouth

QUILLBACK
Carpiodes cyprinus

Other Names: silver carp, carpsucker, lake quillback

Habitat: slow-flowing streams and rivers; backwaters and lakes, particularly areas with soft bottoms

Range: south-central Canada through the Great Lakes to the eastern U.S., south through the Mississippi drainage to the Gulf of Mexico; in New York, the Susquehanna and Allegheny watersheds and lakes Ontario, Erie, Champlain and the St. Lawrence River

Food: insects, plant matter, decaying bottom material

Reproduction: spawns in late spring through early summer in tributaries or lake shallows; eggs are deposited in open areas over sand or mud bottom

Average Size: 12 to 14 inches, 1 to 3 pounds

Records: state—none; North American—8 pounds, 13 ounces, Lake Winnebago, Wisconsin, 2003

Notes: In New York the Quillback is the only representative of the four North American fish known as carpsuckers. Quillbacks prefer medium to large rivers and lakes and even through they are relatively rare in New York, they can be abundant in some waters. They are schooling fish that filter feed along the bottom. Not often sought by anglers, they readily take wet flies and can be very sporting when caught on light tackle. The flesh is white and very flavorful.

Description: dark gray-brown back; yellow to brassy sides; off-white belly; dull red to orange fins and tail; blunt nose; down-turned sucker mouth

Similar Species: Creek Chubsucker (pg. 142), Longnose Sucker (pg. 144), Northern Hog Sucker (pg. 146), White Sucker (pg. 148)

Shorthead Redhorse	**Creek Chubsucker**	**Longnose Sucker**	**White Sucker**
deeply forked, pointed tail	slightly forked, rounded tail	slightly forked, rounded tail	slightly forked, rounded tail

Shorthead Redhorse	**Northern Hog Sucker**
head flat to raised between eyes	head concave between eyes

SHORTHEAD REDHORSE

Catostomidae

Moxostoma macrolepidotum

Other Names: none

Habitat: clean streams and rivers with hard bottoms; clear lakes with strong-flowing tributary streams

Range: central Canada and U.S. through Atlantic states; in New York, lakes Erie and Ontario, and all river drainages except the Delaware, Susquehanna and on Long Island

Food: aquatic insects, small crustaceans, plant debris

Reproduction: spawns from late May to June when the water reaches low 60s F; adults migrate into small tributary streams to lay eggs on shallow gravel bars in swift current near deep pools

Average Size: 18 to 24 inches, 2 to 5 pounds

Records: state—11 pounds, 11 ounces, Salmon River, Oswego County, 1996 (not registered as a North American record); North American—11 pounds, 5 ounces, Brunet River, Wisconsin, 1983

Notes: There are six redhorse species in New York ranging from 2 to 10 pounds. The Shorthead is one of the largest, most common and widespread. All are "sucker-type fish," rather similar in appearance. They are primarily stream fish; the Shorthead Redhorse is the exception, inhabiting lakes as well as streams. They may look similar but each is a separate species. Not of sporting importance but a fairly common catch of river anglers. They fight well on light tackle and are bony but have good flavor when smoked.

Description: olive brown back; yellow to olive sides with dark band that may appear as connected blotches; creamy yellow belly; scales have distinct dark edges

Similar Species: Longnose Sucker (pg. 144), Northern Hog Sucker (pg. 146), White Sucker (pg. 148)

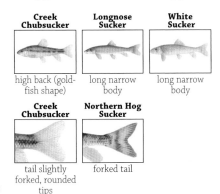

Creek Chubsucker	**Longnose Sucker**	**White Sucker**
high back (goldfish shape)	long narrow body	long narrow body

Creek Chubsucker	**Northern Hog Sucker**
tail slightly forked, rounded tips	forked tail

CREEK CHUBSUCKER

Erimyzon oblongus

Other Names: sweet or yellow sucker

Habitat: sluggish pools of small to medium-size streams and clear lakes

Range: Atlantic coast from north Georgia to Maine; the Mississippi River drainage north to the southern Great Lakes; most drainages in New York

Food: small crustaceans, aquatic insects

Reproduction: spawning takes place in April and May when water reaches the 60s F; a shallow nest is excavated in sand or gravel of small tributary streams; males aggressively defend breeding territories around nest; eggs and young are not guarded

Average Size: 8 to 14 inches

Records: none

Notes: The Creek Chubsucker is one of the most important forage fish in many small New York lakes and streams. Chubsuckers are very prolific and even a small number of breeding adults in a lake produce large numbers of fry for game fish. They survive well on a hook and in the bait pail, making them ideal large bait minnows. Chubsuckers readily take a worm-baited hook and can provide great sport for young kids spending a day on the creek.

Description: back black to dark olive; sides slate gray fading to creamy belly; long snout protrudes beyond upper lip

Similar Species: Creek Chubsucker (pg. 142), Northern Hog Sucker (pg. 146), Shorthead Redhorse (pg. 140), White Sucker (pg. 148)

Longnose Sucker	Northern Hog Sucker	Shorthead Redhorse	White Sucker
snout protrudes beyond mouth	snout does not protrude beyond mouth	snout does not protrude beyond mouth	mouth almost even with snout

Longnose Sucker	Creek Chubsucker
long, narrow body	high back (goldfish shape)

LONGNOSE SUCKER

Catostomus catostomus

Other Names: sturgeon, red or redside sucker

Habitat: deep waters of large, cold, clear lakes and occasionally deep pools of clear streams

Range: Siberia across Canada through the Great Lakes to the eastern U.S., the Missouri and Columbia river systems in the West; common in many deep, clear lakes in New York, not found in Lake Erie

Food: small crustaceans, plant material

Reproduction: spawns during daylight in May and June; adults crowd into fast-flowing tributary streams to deposit eggs over gravel bars; fry move into lakes soon after hatching

Average Size: 15 to 20 inches, 2 pounds

Records: state—none; North American—6 pounds, 14 ounces, St. Joseph River, Michigan, 1986

Notes: The Longnose Sucker is a northern coldwater fish that can be very common in deep, clear lakes. It rarely takes a baited hook but is caught with nets or spears (where legal) during the spawning run. Delicious when smoked and considered by some to surpass the White Sucker in flavor.

Description: back dark olive brown fading to yellow-brown blotches on sides; 4 to 5 irregular dark saddles; elongated body almost round in cross section; large head that is concave between the eyes; lower fins are dull red

Similar Species: Longnose Sucker (pg. 144), Shorthead Redhorse (pg. 140), White Sucker (pg. 148),

Northern Hog Sucker	Longnose Sucker	Shorthead Redhorse	White Sucker
head concave between eyes	head flat to raised between eyes	head flat to raised between eyes	head flat to raised between eyes

NORTHERN HOG SUCKER

Catostomidae

Hypentelium nigricans

Other Names: hog molly, hammerhead, riffle or bigheaded sucker, crawl-a-bottom

Habitat: riffles and tailwaters of clear streams with hard bottoms; found in a few lakes near the mouths of tributary streams

Range: central and eastern Canada and the U.S. south to Alabama, west to Oklahoma; in New York, common in the Great Lakes and western drainages, the Hudson and Susquehanna drainages in the east

Food: small crustaceans, aquatic insects

Reproduction: spawns in April and May when water reaches low 60s F; males gather in riffles or downstream ends of pools; females enter spawning areas just long enough to drop eggs, which are quickly fertilized by several males; no parental care

Average Size: 10 to 12 inches, 1 pound

Records: state—none; North American—1 pound, 12 ounces, Fox River, Wisconsin, 2004

Notes: Northern Hog Suckers are clean-water fish well adapted to feed in moving water. They use their elongated shape and concave head to hold their place in riffles while turning over stones to release food. It is common for other fish to follow Hog Suckers to feed on what is stirred up. Hog Suckers are of not much interest to anglers but are sometimes caught by trout fishermen working the edges of fast water.

Description: olive to brownish back; sides gray to silver; belly off-white; dorsal and tail fin slate; the lower fins tinged orange; snout barely extends beyond upper lip

Similar Species: Longnose Sucker (pg. 144), Northern Hog Sucker (pg. 146), Shorthead Redhorse (pg. 140)

White Sucker

snout barely extends past upper lip

Longnose Sucker

snout extends well beyond upper lip

White Sucker

head flat to raised between eyes

Northern Hog Sucker

concave head between eyes

White Sucker

slightly forked, rounded tail

Shorthead Redhorse

deeply forked, pointed tail

WHITE SUCKER
Catostomus commersonii

Other Names: common, coarse-scaled or eastern sucker, black mullet, bay fish

Habitat: clear to turbid (cloudy) streams, rivers and lakes

Range: Canada through central and eastern U.S. south to a line from New Mexico to South Carolina; common in most New York waters

Food: insects, crustaceans, plant matter

Reproduction: spawns in early spring when water reaches high 50s to low 60s F; adults spawn in tributary riffles over gravel or coarse sand; in lakes, eggs are deposited over shallow gravel or rocks along wave-swept shorelines

Average Size: 12 to 18 inches, 1 to 3 pounds

Records: state—5 pounds, 3 ounces, Hudson River, Warren County, 1994; North American—7 pounds, 4 ounces, Big Round Lake, Wisconsin, 1978

Notes: The White Sucker is one of the most common fish in New York and one of the most important. Highly productive, it provides a large source of forage for game fish and is a mainstay in the bait industry. They are not the great consumers of trout eggs they were once thought to be but may compete with trout fry for food when first hatched. The tremendous forage source young White Suckers provide for game fish offsets this competition. White Suckers are most often fished during the spring spawning run. The flesh is firm and good tasting.

149

Description: dark green back; greenish sides often with dark lateral band; belly white to gray; large forward-facing mouth; lower jaw extends to rear margin of eye

Similar Species: Smallmouth Bass (pg. 152)

Largemouth Bass

mouth extends well beyond non-red eye

Smallmouth Bass

mouth does not extend beyond red eye

150

LARGEMOUTH BASS

Micropterus salmoides

Centrarchidae

Other Names: black, bayou, green or slough bass, green trout

Habitat: shallow, fertile, weedy lakes and river backwaters; weedy bays and extensive weedbeds of large lakes

Range: southern Canada through United States into Mexico, extensively introduced worldwide; common throughout New York

Food: small fish, frogs, insects, crayfish

Reproduction: spawns when water temperatures reach 60 degrees F; male builds nest in small clearings in weedbeds 2 to 8 feet deep, then guards nest and fry until the "brood swarm" disperses

Average Size: 12 to 20 inches, 1 to 5 pounds

Records: state—11 pounds, 4 ounces, Buckhorn Lake, Otsego County, 1987; North American—22 pounds, 4 ounces, Montgomery Lake, Georgia, 1932

Notes: Largemouth Bass are the most sought-after game fish in North America. These denizens of the weedbeds are voracious carnivores and eat anything that is alive and will fit into their mouth. Largemouths are common in New York lakes and large streams that have weedbeds in less than 20 feet of water. Largemouth Bass often run 1 to 2 pounds with 5 pounders not uncommon in New York. They are good to eat when small and from clean water, but tend to be slightly muddy flavored when taken from silty water.

Description: back and sides mottled dark green to bronze or pale gold, often with dark vertical bands; white belly; stout body; large, forward-facing mouth; red eye

Similar Species: Largemouth Bass (pg. 150)

Smallmouth Bass
mouth does not extend beyond red eye

Largemouth Bass
mouth extends well beyond non-red eye

SMALLMOUTH BASS

Micropterus dolomieu

Centrarchidae

Other Names: bronzeback, brown or redeye bass, redeye

Habitat: clear, swift-flowing streams and rivers; clear lakes with gravel or rocky shorelines

Range: extensively introduced across North America, Europe and Asia; common in the Great Lakes and New York

Food: insects, small fish, crayfish

Reproduction: male builds nest in 3 to 10 feet of water (may be up to 20 feet in the clear waters of Lake Erie) on open gravel beds when water temperatures reach mid to high 60s F; nest is often near logs or boulders; male aggressively guards the nest and young until fry disperse

Average Size: 12 to 20 inches, 1 to 4 pounds

Records: state—8 pounds, 4 ounces, Lake Erie, Chautauqua County, 1995; North American—11 pounds, 15 ounces, Dale Hollow Lake, Tennessee, 1955

Notes: Smallmouth Bass are world-class game fish noted for their strong fights and high jumps. Native to New York, they have been extensively introduced throughout the world and though the range of this slow-maturing fish has expanded, its numbers are decreasing due to overfishing and habitat loss. Avoiding weedbeds, Smallmouth Bass prefer deeper, more open water than their big cousin the Largemouth Bass. The flesh is firm, succulent and regarded by some as second only to Lake Trout and Whitefish.

Description: black to olive back; silver sides with dark green to black blotches; back more arched and depression above eye more pronounced than White Crappie

Similar Species: White Crappie (pg. 156)

Black Crappie	White Crappie	Black Crappie	White Crappie
usually 7 to 8 spines in dorsal fin	usually 5 to 6 spines in dorsal fin	dorsal fin length equal to distance from dorsal to eye	dorsal fin shorter than distance from eye to dorsal

BLACK CRAPPIE
Pomoxis nigromaculatus

Other Names: speckled perch, speck, papermouth

Habitat: quiet, clear water of streams and mid-sized lakes; often associated with vegetation but may roam deep, open basins and flats, particularly during winter

Range: southern Manitoba through Atlantic and southeastern states, introduced but not common in the West; common throughout New York

Food: small fish, aquatic insects, zooplankton

Reproduction: spawns in shallow weedbeds from May to June when water temperatures reach the high 50s F; male builds circular nest in fine gravel or sand and then guards the eggs and young until fry begin feeding

Average Size: 7 to 12 inches, 5 ounces to 1 pound

Records: state—3 pounds, 12 ounces, Duck Lake, Cayuga County, 1998; North American—6 pounds, Westwego Canal, Louisiana, 1969

Notes: The Black Crappie is the most widespread crappie in New York and is found in most lakes that have clear water and good weed growth. Seldom found in moving water. They are the most popular New York panfish in all seasons, actively feeding winter and summer. Black Crappies are sought for their sweet-tasting white fillets, not their fighting ability. They nest in colonies and often gather in large feeding schools. Black Crappies require clearer water and more vegetation than White Crappies.

Description: greenish back; silvery green to white sides with 7 to 9 dark vertical bars; the only sunfish with six spines in both the dorsal and anal fin

Similar Species: Black Crappie (pg. 154)

White Crappie	Black Crappie	White Crappie	Black Crappie
usually 5 to 6 spines in dorsal fin	usually 7 to 8 spines in dorsal fin	dorsal fin shorter than distance from eye to dorsal	dorsal fin length equal to distance from dorsal to eye

WHITE CRAPPIE

Pomoxis annularis

Other Names: silver, pale or ringed crappie, papermouth

Habitat: slightly silty streams and mid-size lakes; prefers less vegetation than Black Crappie

Range: North Dakota south and east to the Gulf and Atlantic states except peninsular Florida; common across New York

Food: aquatic insects, zooplankton, small fish

Reproduction: spawns on firm sand or gravel bottom when water temperatures approach 60 degrees F; male builds shallow, round nest, guards eggs and young after spawning

Average Size: 8 to 10 inches, 5 to 16 ounces

Records: state—3 pounds, 13 ounces, Sleepy Hollow Lake, Greene County, 2001; North American—5 pounds, 3 ounces, Enid Dam, Mississippi, 1957

Notes: White Crappies, the southern cousin to Black Crappies, are native to western New York and are now common throughout the state. They prefer deeper, less weedy, and more turbid (cloudy) water than Black Crappies and are not as common. Due to its acceptance of turbid water there is some indication of a positive relationship between the Common Carp and White Crappie. Black and White Crappies can be found in mixed schools in winter and occasionally hybridize. Both actively feed during the winter and at night.

Description: dark olive to green on back, blending to silver-gray, copper, orange, purple or brown on sides; 5 to 9 dark vertical bars on sides that fade with age; yellow belly and copper breast; large, dark gill spot; dark spot on dorsal fin

Similar Species: Green Sunfish (pg. 162), Pumpkinseed (pg. 164), Redbreast Sunfish (pg. 166)

Bluegill

dark gill spot on rounded gill flap

Pumpkinseed

red/orange crescent on gill spot

Redbreast Sunfish

long, narrow gill flap

Bluegill

small mouth

Green Sunfish

large mouth

158

BLUEGILL

Lepomis macrochirus

Other Names: bream, sun perch, blue sunfish, copperbelly, strawberry bass

Habitat: medium to large streams and most lakes with weedy bays or shorelines

Range: southern Canada through the southern states into Mexico; common throughout New York

Food: aquatic insects, snails, small fish

Reproduction: spawns from late May to early August when water temperatures reach the high 60s to low 80s F; male builds nest in shallow, sparse vegetation in colony of up to 50 other nests; male guards nest and fry

Average Size: 6 to 9 inches, 5 to 8 ounces

Records: state—2 pounds, 8 ounces, Kohlbach Pond, Broome County, 1992; North American—4 pounds, 12 ounces, Ketona Lake, Alabama, 1950

Notes: Bluegills are the most popular panfish in New York and throughout the United States. They have small mouths and feed mostly on insects and small fish. They often feed on the surface and are popular with fly fishermen. Bluegills prefer deep weedbeds at the edge of open water. Many lakes have large populations of hybrid sunfish, crosses between Bluegills and Green or Pumpkinseed Sunfish.

Description: dark olive to black back and sides fading to light olive belly; blue-green spots run in lines down sides; small dark gill spot; tail rounded

Similar Species: Pumpkinseed (pg. 164), Redbreasted Sunfish (pg. 166)

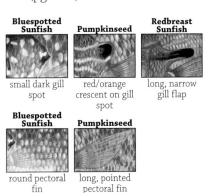

Bluespotted Sunfish	Pumpkinseed	Redbreast Sunfish
small dark gill spot	red/orange crescent on gill spot	long, narrow gill flap

Bluespotted Sunfish	Pumpkinseed
round pectoral fin	long, pointed pectoral fin

BLUESPOTTED SUNFISH

Enneacanthus gloriosus

Other Names: spotted or bluedot sunfish

Habitat: shallow, weedy lakes and river backwaters

Range: Atlantic drainage from southern New York to Florida; southeastern New York

Food: aquatic insects, crustaceans

Reproduction: spawns in May and June when water temperatures reach the high 60s F; male builds small, round nest in weedbeds and defends the nest and young

Average Size: 3 to 4 inches

Records: none

Notes: This is a common, small sunfish found in freshwater along the eastern seaboard. Bluespotted Sunfish are not large enough to be of any value to anglers but are prolific and an important forage fish for larger game fish. They can occupy water lower in oxygen than other sunfish and may be very important in mosquito control in some areas. The breeding males are brightly colored and make great aquarium fish (where legal).

Description: dark green back with dark olive to bluish sides; yellow to cream belly; scales flecked with yellow, producing a brassy appearance; dark gill spot with light margin; large mouth and thick lips

Similar Species: Bluegill (pg. 158), Pumpkinseed (pg. 164), Redbreast Sunfish (pg. 166)

Green Sunfish	Bluegill	Pumpkinseed	Redbreast Sunfish
prominent, light margin on rounded gill spot	dark gill spot	red/orange crescent on gill spot	long, narrow gill flap

GREEN SUNFISH
Lepomis cyanellus

Other Names: green perch, sand bass

Habitat: warm, weedy, shallow lakes and the backwaters of slow-moving streams

Range: most of the U.S. into Mexico excluding Florida and the Rocky Mountains; found throughout New York

Food: aquatic insects, small crustaceans, fish

Reproduction: male builds nest in less than a foot of weedy water, in temperatures from 60 to 80 degrees F; may produce two broods per year; male guards nest and fans eggs till hatching

Average Size: 4 to 6 inches, less than 8 ounces

Records: state—none; North American—2 pounds, 2 ounces, Stockton Lake, Missouri, 1971

Notes: Green Sunfish are often mistaken for Bluegills but prefer shallower weedbeds. They are native to western New York and are now found throughout the state but are not very common. Green Sunfish can be abundant in one pond and absent from the one next to it. Green Sunfish sometimes hybridize with Bluegills and Pumpkinseeds, producing large, aggressive offspring; they may also "stunt," filling a pond with half-dollar-size breeding fish.

Description: back brown to olive fading to light olive; orange-yellow spots on sides, with 7 to 10 vertical bands; black gill spot with light margin and orange or red crescent

Similar Species: Bluegill (pg. 158), Green Sunfish (pg. 162), Redbreast Sunfish (pg. 166)

Pumpkinseed	**Green Sunfish**	**Pumpkinseed**	**Green Sunfish**
small mouth	large mouth	long, pointed pectoral fin	short, round pectoral fin

Pumpkinseed	**Bluegill**
orange or red crescent on gill flap	gill flap lacks orange or red margin

PUMPKINSEED

Lepomis gibbosus

Centrarchidae

Other Names: yellow or round sunfish, sun bass, bream

Habitat: weedy ponds, clear lakes, reservoirs and slow moving streams; prefers slightly cooler water than Bluegill

Range: central and eastern North America, introduced in the West; common throughout New York

Food: snails, aquatic and terrestrial insects, small fish

Reproduction: spawns from late May to August when water temperatures reach 55 to 63 degrees F; male builds nest among weeds in less than two feet of water over sand or gravel bottom; male aggressively guards the nest; may produce multiple broods

Average Size: 6 to 8 inches, 5 to 8 ounces

Records: state—1 pound, 9 ounces, Indian Lake, Hamilton County, 1994; North American—2 pounds, 4 ounces, North Saluda River, South Carolina, 1997

Notes: This small, brightly colored sunfish is one of the most well-known and beautiful fish native to New York. Pumpkinseeds often gather in small schools around docks and submerged deadfalls. They prefer slightly cooler and more open water than Bluegills. They readily hybridize with other sunfish, with the hybrids totally colonizing some lakes. Pumpkinseeds commonly "stunt," filling lakes with $2^1/_2$-inch breeding adults. Has specialized teeth for feeding on snails. Eagerly attacks small natural and artificial bait and provides fine table fare.

165

Description: dark olive-green back; olive sides; gray-white belly; bright yellow-orange breast; gill flap long, black and narrower than eye; tail slightly forked

Similar Species: Bluegill (pg. 158), Bluespotted Sunfish (pg. 160), Pumpkinseed (pg. 164)

Redbreast Sunfish	Bluegill	Pumpkinseed
short round pectoral fin	long, pointed pectoral fin	long, pointed pectoral fin

Redbreast Sunfish	Bluespotted Sunfish	Pumpkinseed
long, narrow, dark gill flap	small, dark gill spot	orange or red crescent

REDBREAST SUNFISH
Lepomis auritus

Other Names: yellowbelly or longear sunfish, sun perch, redbreast bream

Habitat: rocky riffles in streams with medium current, occasionally lakes or reservoirs

Range: Atlantic drainage from southern New York to Florida; southeastern New York

Food: aquatic insects, crustaceans, small fish

Reproduction: spawns in May and June when water temperatures reach the high 60s F; male builds small, round nest in weedbeds away from the current; male defends nest

Average Size: 4 to 8 inches, 4 ounces

Records: state—none; North American—2 pounds, 1 ounce, Suwannee River, Florida, 1988

Notes: This is a common, small to medium-size sunfish native to the Atlantic drainage east of the Alleghenies. It prefers streams but is often found in reservoirs and lakes. Redbreast Sunfish frequent the same habitat as Smallmouth Bass and Rock Bass. In New York, this solitary sunfish is too small to be popular with anglers but is aggressive and often takes bait.

Description: brown to olive green back and sides with overall bronze appearance; each scale on sides has a dark spot; red eye; thicker, heavier body than other sunfish; large mouth

Similar Species: Bluegill (pg. 158), Green Sunfish (pg. 162)

Rock Bass	Bluegill	Rock Bass	Green Sunfish
large mouth extends to eye	small mouth does not extend to eye	6 spines in anal fin	3 spines in anal fin

ROCK BASS

Ambloplites rupestris

Centrarchidae

Other Names: redeye, goggle eye, rock sunfish

Habitat: vegetation on firm to rocky bottom in clear lakes and medium-size streams

Range: southern Canada through central and eastern U.S. to the northern edge of the Gulf States; common throughout New York

Food: prefers crayfish; also eats aquatic insects, small fish

Reproduction: spawns when water temperatures reach high 60s to 70s F; male builds nest in coarse gravel in submerged vegetation less than 3 feet deep; male guards eggs and fry

Average Size: 8 to 10 inches, 8 ounces to 1 pound

Records: state—1 pound, 15 ounces, Ramapo River, Rockland County, 1984; North American—3 pounds, York River, Ontario, 1974

Notes: A large sunfish native to western New York but now common throughout the state. It is plentiful, a good fighter and often caught but not often sought by fishermen. Its flesh is somewhat stronger flavored than that of Bluegills. In both lakes and streams, Rock Bass are normally found over a rocky or gravel substrate even when vegetation is present. Rock Bass are frequently found in schools that stay put, not moving from their home territories. Once these schools are located, Rock Bass are easy to catch.

Description: gray-black back; silver sides with 6 to 8 uninter-rupted black stripes; front of dorsal fin separated from soft-rayed rear portion; lower jaw protrudes beyond snout

Similar Species: Striped Bass Hybrid (pg. 172), Striped Bass (pg. 174), White Perch (pg. 176)

single spine on gill cover

two spines on gill cover

horizontal black stripes

no stripes except lateral line

single tooth patch on tongue

two tooth patches on tongue

two tooth patches on tongue

WHITE BASS

Morone chrysops

Moronidae

Other Names: lake, sand or silver bass, streaker

Habitat: large lakes, rivers and impoundments with relatively clear water

Range: Great Lakes region to the eastern seaboard, through the southeast to the Gulf and west to Texas; in New York, the Great Lakes and a few large impoundments

Food: small fish, insects, crustaceans

Reproduction: spawns in late spring or early summer; eggs spread in open water over gravel beds or rubble 6 to 10 feet deep; some populations migrate to narrow bays or up tributary streams to spawn

Average Size: 9 to 18 inches, 8 ounces to 2 pounds

Records: state—3 pounds, 6 ounces, Furnace Brook, Westchester County, 1992; North American—6 pounds, 7 ounces, Saginaw Bay, Michigan, 1989

Notes: The White Bass is native to the Great Lakes and has been stocked in other New York lakes. It inhabits large lakes and rivers, traveling in large schools near the surface. White Bass can often be spotted by watching for seagulls feeding on baitfish driven to the surface. Anglers often gather in large numbers along streams during the spawning run. The flesh is somewhat soft but has a good flavor. Both can be improved if fish are put on ice and chilled as soon as they are caught.

Description: dark gray back; bright silver sides with 7 or 8 indistinct or broken stripes; dorsal fin separated, front part has hard spines, rear part has soft rays; two tooth patches, one on back of tongue

Similar Species: Striped Bass (pg. 174), White Bass (pg. 170), White Perch (pg. 176)

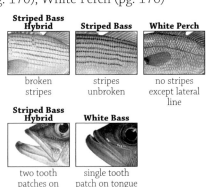

Striped Bass Hybrid

broken stripes

Striped Bass

stripes unbroken

White Perch

no stripes except lateral line

Striped Bass Hybrid

two tooth patches on tongue

White Bass

single tooth patch on tongue

STRIPED BASS HYBRID

Morone saxatilis x Morone chrysops

Moronidae

Other Names: white striper, whiterock, wiper

Habitat: open water of large lakes and slow-moving rivers

Range: stocked in about 40 U.S. states; stocked in a few New York lakes

Food: small fish, insects, crustaceans

Reproduction: hatchery-produced hybrid that is only occasionally fertile

Average Size: 1 to 2 feet, 5 to 10 pounds

Records: state—15 pounds, 5 ounces, Lake Waccabuc, Westchester County, 2004; North American—27 pounds, 5 ounces, Greers Ferry Lake, Arkansas, 1997

Notes: The Striped Bass Hybrid is a hatchery cross normally between a female Striped Bass and a male White Bass. It does not reproduce but may back-cross with the parent stock. New York raises large numbers of fingerlings to stock in impoundments too warm to support Striped Bass. This hard-fighting, tasty hybrid has become a favorite of anglers in New York and across the country. It is also becoming an important aquaculture fish, supplying fillets for the grocery and restaurant market.

Description: dark gray back; bright silver sides with 7 or 8 distinct stripes; jaw protrudes beyond snout; dorsal fin separated, front part hard spines, rear part soft rays

Similar Species: White Bass (pg. 170), Striped Bass Hybrid (pg. 172), White Perch (pg. 176)

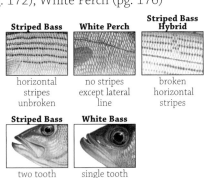

Striped Bass	White Perch	Striped Bass Hybrid
horizontal stripes unbroken	no stripes except lateral line	broken horizontal stripes

Striped Bass	White Bass
two tooth patches on tongue	single tooth patch on tongue

STRIPED BASS

Moronidae

Morone saxatilis

Other Names: striper, streaker, surf bass, rockfish

Habitat: coastal oceans and associated spawning streams; landlocked in some large lakes and reservoirs

Range: Atlantic coast from Maine to northern Florida, Gulf Coast from Florida to Texas; introduced elsewhere; coastal New York and Hudson River

Food: small fish

Reproduction: spawns in late spring to early summer in freshwater streams; eggs deposited in riffles over gravel bars at the mouth of large tributaries; eggs must remain suspended to hatch

Average Size: 18 to 30 inches, 10 to 20 pounds

Records: state—55 pounds, 6 ounces, Hudson River, Ulster County, 2007; North American—(inland) 67 pounds, 1 ounce, Colorado River, Arizona, 1997; (marine)—78 pounds, 8 ounces, Atlantic City, New Jersey, 1992 (IGFA)

Notes: The Striped Bass is a saltwater fish that migrates into freshwater to spawn, mainly in the Hudson River in New York. Striped Bass can be reared in hatcheries and are now stocked into many large southern and western lakes and rivers. These populations cannot reproduce naturally and must be maintained through stocking programs. The most renowned Striped Bass fishery is along the Atlantic coast from New York to the Carolinas, but a second important fishery is developing in inland lakes and rivers.

Description: olive to blackish green back; silver-green sides with no stripes; front spiny dorsal fin connected by small low membrane to soft ray back portion

Similar Species: Striped Bass (pg. 174), White Bass (pg. 170), Striped Bass Hybrid (pg. 172)

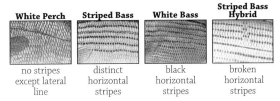

White Perch	Striped Bass	White Bass	Striped Bass Hybrid
no stripes except lateral line	distinct horizontal stripes	black horizontal stripes	broken horizontal stripes

WHITE PERCH

Morone americana

Other Names: narrow-mouth bass, silver or sea perch

Habitat: brackish water in coastal areas; near-shore areas of the Great Lakes; expanding range into smaller freshwater lakes

Range: Mississippi River drainage south to the Gulf of Mexico, Atlantic coast from Maine to South Carolina; in New York, Lake Ontario and coastal waters, expanding range into central New York lakes

Food: fish eggs in spring and early summer; minnows, insects, crustaceans

Reproduction: spawns in late spring over gravel bars of tributary streams

Average Size: 6 to 8 inches, 1 pound or less

Records: state—3 pounds, 1 ounce, Lake Oscaletta, Westchester County, 1991; North American—4 pounds, 12 ounces, Messalonskee Lake, Maine, 1949

Notes: The White Perch is a coastal Atlantic species that entered the Great Lakes in the 1950s. The inland form of this brackish water fish is quickly expanding its range, often in places were it is unwanted. Fish eggs make up 100 percent of its diet in the spring and it has been linked to Walleye declines in some Canadian waters. White Perch are a popular panfish in some parts of the Great Lakes and are commercially harvested in western Lake Erie but are a detriment in many smaller lakes.

Description: olive to brown back; sides yellow-brown; dark lateral bands; slender with pelvic, dorsal and anal fins set well back on body; long snout flattened on top; rounded tail; upturned mouth

Similar Species: Brook Silversides (pg. 127), Central Mudminnow (pg. 78)

Banded Killifish	Brook Silversides	Banded Killifish	Central Mudminnow
single dorsal fin	two dorsal fins	lacks dark bar or blotch below eye	dark bar or blotch below eye

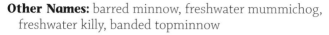

BANDED KILLIFISH

Fundulus diaphanus

Other Names: barred minnow, freshwater mummichog, freshwater killy, banded topminnow

Habitat: still pools in slow-moving streams; shoal waters of large lakes and brackish estuaries

Range: maritime provinces of Canada south through the Carolinas, west to Idaho; common across New York

Food: insects, crustaceans

Reproduction: spawns when water reaches low 70s F; female lays 1 to 30 eggs suspended on long filament; eggs are fertilized while still attached to female, then drop to bottom to hatch unattended

Average Size: 2 to 3 inches

Records: none

Notes: As the family name implies, "topminnows" inhabit the upper water column and are adapted to feeding on or near the surface. Though inconspicuous and well camouflaged they are a favorite target of wading birds. Banded Killifish are widespread in New York, living in fresh- and saltwater. They can withstand low oxygen levels and are often used as bait minnows—even farmed in Michigan for this purpose. Though not very colorful, they make good aquarium fish that readily eat food spread on the water surface.

Description: silvery brown back and sides; horizontal rows of dark blotches; adipose fin; single dorsal fin with 2 weak spines and 10 to 11 soft rays; small scales that feel rough

Similar Species: Yellow Perch (pg. 88), Walleye (pg. 86)

Trout-perch	Yellow Perch	Walleye
adipose fin	lacks adipose fin	lacks adipose fin

TROUT-PERCH

Percopsis omiscomaycus

Other Names: grounder, sand minnow

Habitat: clear to slightly turbid (cloudy) deep lakes and streams with sand or gravel bottom; avoids soft-bottomed shallows

Range: east-central U.S. south to Kansas and Canada west to Alaska; in New York, the Great Lakes, St. Lawrence, Hudson and Allegheny drainages

Food: insects, zooplankton, crustaceans, small fish

Reproduction: migrates from deep water to shorelines and tributary streams when water temperatures reach the high 60s F; spawns over gravel or rocks, leaving eggs to hatch with no parental care

Average Size: 2 to 4 inches

Records: none

Notes: There are only two species of Trout-perch and they are restricted to freshwater in North America. Trout-perch are deep-water fish seldom seen unless they wash up on a beach, where they are often confused with small Walleyes. They have a nocturnal migration and some nights large numbers enter the shallows to feed. Trout-perch are an important forage species for game fish and can be a good baitfish. However, seining is only productive in shallow water at night.

GLOSSARY

adipose fin a small, fleshy fin without rays, located on the midline of the fish's back between the dorsal fin and the tail

air bladder a balloon-like organ located in the gut area of a fish, used to control buoyancy—and in the respiration of some species such as gar; also called "swim bladder" or "gas bladder"

alevin a newly hatched fish that still has its yolk sac

anadromous a fish that hatches in freshwater, migrates to the ocean, then re-enters streams or rivers from the sea (or large inland body of water) to spawn

anal fin a single fin located on the underside near the tail

annulus marks or rings on the scales, spine, vertebrae or otoliths that scientists use to determine a fish's age

anterior toward the front of a fish, opposite of posterior

bands horizontal markings running lengthwise along the side of a fish

barbel thread-like sensory structures on a fish's head often near the mouth, commonly called "whiskers"; used for taste or smell

bars vertical markings on the side of a fish

benthic organisms living in or on the bottom of a body of water

brood swarm a large group or "cloud" of young fish such as Black Bullheads

carnivore a predatory fish that feeds on other fish (also called a piscivore) or animals

catadromous a fish that lives in freshwater and migrates into saltwater to spawn, such as the American Eel

caudal fin the tail or tail fin

caudal peduncle the portion of the fish's body located between the anal fin and the beginning of the tail

coldwater referring to a species or environment; in fish, often a species of trout or salmon found in water that rarely exceeds 70 degrees F; also used to describe a lake or river according to average summer temperature

copepod a small (less than 2 mm) crustacean, part of the zooplankton community

crustacean a crayfish, water flea, crab or other animal belonging to group of mostly aquatic species that have paired antennae, jointed legs and an exterior skeleton (exoskeleton); common food for many fish

dorsal relating to the top of the fish, on or near the back; opposite of the ventral, or lower, part of the fish

dorsal fin the fin or fins located along the top of a fish's back

eddy a circular water current, often created by an obstruction

epilimnion the warm, oxygen-rich upper layer of water in a thermally stratified lake

exotic a foreign species, not native to a watershed, such as the Zebra Mussel

fingerling a juvenile fish, generally 1 to 10 inches in length, in its first year of life

fork length the overall length of fish from mouth to the deepest part of the tail notch

fry recently hatched young fish that have already absorbed their yolk sacs

game fish a species regulated by laws for recreational fishing

gills organs used in aquatic respiration (breathing)

gill cover large bone covering the fish's gills, also called opercle or operculum

gill flap also called ear flap; fleshy projection on the back edge of the gill cover of some fish such as Bluegill

gill raker a comblike projection from the gill arch

harvest fish that are caught and kept by recreational or commercial anglers

hypolimnion bottom layer of the water column in a thermally stratified lake (common in summer); usually depleted of oxygen by decaying matter and inhospitable to most fish

ichthyologist a scientist who studies fish

invertebrates animals without backbones, such as insects, leeches and earthworms

kype hooked jaw acquired by some trout and salmon mainly during breeding season

lateral line a series of pored scales along the side of a fish that contain organs used to detect vibrations

littoral zone the part of a lake that is less than 15 feet in depth; this important and often vulnerable area holds the majority of aquatic plants, is a primary area used by young fish, and offers essential spawning habitat for most warmwater fishes such as Walleye and Largemouth Bass

mandible lower jaw

maxillary upper jaw

milt semen of a male fish that fertilizes the female's eggs during the spawning process

mollusk an invertebrate with a smooth, soft body such as a clam or a snail, often having an outer shell

native an indigenous or naturally occurring species

omnivore a fish or animal that eats plants and animal matter

otolith calcium concentration found in the inner ear of fish; used to determine age of some fish; also called ear bone

opercle the bone covering the gills, also called the gill cover or operculum

panfish small freshwater game fish that can be fried whole in a pan, such as Black Crappie, Bluegill and Yellow Perch

pectoral fins paired fins on the side of the fish located just behind the gills

pelagic fish species that live in open water, in the food-rich upper layer of the column; not associated with the bottom

pelvic fins paired fins located below or behind the pectoral fins on the bottom (ventral portion) of the fish

pheromone a chemical scent secreted as a means of communication between members of the same species

piscivore a predatory fish that mainly eats other fish

planktivore a fish that feeds on plankton

plankton floating or weakly swimming aquatic plants and animals, including larval fish, that drift with the current; often eaten by fish; individual organisms are called plankters

plankton bloom a marked increase in the amount of plankton due to favorable conditions such as nutrients and light

range the geographic region in which a species is found

ray, hard stiff fin support; resembles a spine but is jointed

ray, soft flexible fin support, sometimes branched

redd a nest-like depression made by a male or female fish during the spawn, often refers to nest of trout and salmon species

riprap rock or concrete used to protect a lakeshore or river's bank from erosion

roe fish eggs

scales small, flat plates covering the outer skin of many fish

Secchi disc an 8- to 12-inch-diameter, black-and-white circular disc used to measure water clarity; scientists record the average depth at which the disc disappears from sight when lowered into the water

silt small, easily disturbed bottom particles smaller than sand but larger than clay

siltation the accumulation of soil particles

spawning the process of fish reproduction; involves females laying eggs and males fertilizing them to produce young fish

spine stiff, non-jointed structures found along with soft rays in some fins

spiracle an opening on the posterior portion of the head above and behind the eye

standard length length of the fish from the mouth to the end of the vertebral column

stocking the purposeful, artificial introduction of a fish species into a body of water

substrate bottom composition of a lake, stream or river

subterminal mouth a mouth below the snout of the fish

swim bladder see air bladder

tailrace area of water immediately downstream of a dam or power plant

thermocline middle layer of water in a stratified lake, typically oxygen rich, characterized by a sharp drop in temperature; often the lowest depth at which fish can be routinely found

184

terminal mouth forward facing

total length length of fish from the mouth to the tail compressed to its fullest length

tributary a stream that feeds into another stream, river or lake

turbid cloudy; water clouded by suspended sediments or plant matter that limits visibility and the passage of light

velocity the speed of water flowing in a stream or river

vent the opening at the end of the digestive tract

ventral the underside of the fish

vertebrate an animal with a backbone

warmwater a non-salmonid species of fish that lives in water that routinely exceeds 70 degrees F; also used to describe a lake or river according to average summer temperature

yolk the part of an egg containing food for the developing fish

zooplankton the animal component of plankton; tiny animals that float or swim weakly; common food for small fish

INDEX

186

187

PRIMARY REFERENCES

Becker, G. C. 1983
Fishes of Wisconsin
University of Wisconsin Press

Hubbs, C. L. and Lagler, K. F. revised by Smith, G. R 2004
Fishes of the Great Lakes Region
University of Michigan Press

McClane, A.J. 1978
Freshwater Fishes of North America
Henry Holt and Company

Smith, C. L. 1985
The Inland Fishes of New York State
New York State Department of Environmental Conservation

Thomas, P. assisted by Callahan, E. 2004
Lake Erie Fish Illustrated
Allegheny Press Science Series No. 28

Werner, R. G. 2004
Freshwater Fishes of the Northeastern States
Syracuse University Press

ABOUT THE AUTHOR

Dave Bosanko was born in Kansas and studied engineering before following his love of nature to degrees in biology and chemistry from Emporia State University. He spent thirty years as a staff biologist at two of the University of Minnesota's field stations. Though his training was in mammal physiology, Dave worked on a wide range of research projects ranging from fish, bird and mammal population studies to experiments with biodiversity and prairie restoration. An avid fisherman and naturalist, he has long enjoyed applying the fruits of his extensive field research to patterning fish location and behavior, and observing how these fascinating species interact with one another in the underwater web of life.